practical
·········· ✦ ··········
magic

A Beginner's Guide to

CRYSTALS,

HOROSCOPES,

PSYCHICS

& SPELLS

NIKKI VAN DE CAR

Illustrations by KATIE VERNON

RUNNING PRESS
PHILADELPHIA

Published by Running Press,
An Imprint of Perseus Books, LLC,
A Subsidiary of Hachette Book Group, Inc.

Printed in China
1010

Books published by Running Press are available at special discounts for bulk purchases in the United States by corporations, institutions, and other organizations. For more information, please contact the Special Markets Department at Perseus Books, 2300 Chestnut Street, Suite 200, Philadelphia, PA 19103, or call (800) 810-4145, ext. 5000, or e-mail special.markets@perseusbooks.com.

ISBN 978-0-7624-6307-7
Library of Congress Control Number: 2017939298

E-book ISBN 978-0-7624-6308-4

12
Digit on the right indicates the number of this printing

Edited by Shannon Lee Connors
Designed by Susan Van Horn
Typography: Verlag, Artisania, Filosofia, and Mr Moustache

Running Press Book Publishers
2300 Chestnut Street
Philadelphia, PA 19103-4371

www.runningpress.com

TABLE OF CONTENTS

Introduction . . . 7

PART 1

✴

HEALING FOR HEDGE WITCHES . . . 9

chakras . . . 11

The Seven Chakras . . . 13
Balancing Your Chakras As a Whole . . . 17
Balancing the Individual Chakras . . . 18

crystals . . . 21

The Most Common Stones and Their Uses . . . 23
How to Choose and Activate Your Crystal . . . 25

auras . . . 29

Common Aural Colors and Their Meanings . . . 32
How to See Auras . . . 36
How to Cleanse Your Aura . . . 36

PART 2

✳

MAGIC FOR THE WEEKEND WICCAN...39

healing with herbs...41

Common Herbs and Their Uses...43

How to Make a Tincture...52

How to Make Herbal Oil...52

How to Make a Poultice...53

plant-based magic...55

Common Plants and Their Uses in Magic...57

How to Make a Smudge Stick...60

How to Make a Gris-Gris...61

pagan holidays...63

Samhain...65

Yule...66

Imbolc...68

Ostara...69

Beltane...71

Litha...72

Lammas...73

Mabon...75

white magic...77

The Parts of a Spell...78

Basic Spells...80

PART 3

✴

CASUAL CLAIRVOYANCE... 87

tarot ... 89

The Suits ... 91
The Major Arcana ... 94
Three-Card Spread ... 98
Guidance Spread ... 99

astrology ... 101

The Elements and Their Signs ... 103
The Celestial Bodies ... 107
The Twelve Houses ... 110
How to Create a Natal Chart ... 112

palmistry ... 115

Chiromancy ... 117
Chirognomy ... 124
How to Do a Reading ... 127

dream interpretation ... 129

Common Dream Symbols ... 131
Less Common (But Still Fairly Common) Dream Symbols ... 133
How to Interpret Dreams ... 135
Lucid Dreams ... 136

Conclusion ... 139
References and Resources ... 141
Acknowledgments ... 145
Creating Your Natal Chart ... 146
Index ... 148

INTRODUCTION

DID YOU EVER WONDER WHAT ALL THOSE JARS IN AN OLD apothecary shop hold? And what do they do? Have you ever been just a little bit tempted to learn what a $20 psychic might say about your new job or that fun date you just had? What was your unconscious trying to tell you with that strange dream last night? What *are* chakras, anyway?

This is a book for the occult-curious. It's for anyone who has ever thought, "Hey, why not?" and bought an amethyst because it was pretty, but also because it *just might* bring peace and lucid dreaming. This book is for everyone who finds their daily horoscope weirdly accurate and for anyone who has always secretly wanted to live in a world of magic.

Here you'll learn the basics of crystal healing, herb magic, and palmistry. You'll learn how to cast a few basic spells (all white magic, of course!), see auras, and throw a proper Beltane party. You'll learn how to interpret your dreams, cleanse your chakras, and chart your stars.

Mostly, you'll laugh and have fun. But maybe, just maybe, you'll experience something surprising. That odd feeling of discomfort you have when you stand in that one corner of your apartment might just vanish with a little light sage-smudging. You might find that an eerily accurate tarot reading will cause you to make a slightly different choice than you might otherwise have or will give you the courage to have faith in yourself and what's to come. Maybe, for fun, you'll cast a love spell over your friend before she goes to meet her blind date, and they'll hit it off like crazy. It might be just a tingle, a hint of the supernatural, something unexplainable but undeniable.

Here's the thing—you don't have to believe in magic to enjoy this book. You just have to want to.

PART 1

✶

HEALING FOR HEDGE WITCHES

*Chakras, crystals, and auras . . .
look deep within, and expand your
inner eye to explore beyond.*

CHAKRAS

. . . .

FOR A WHILE THERE, OUR IMPRESSION OF ANYONE WHO WAS interested in chakras was that they were just weird and kind of silly. But nowadays more of us are taking them seriously. There is a long history here, found in many cultures around the globe, and there's actually some real science behind it all.

We all understand and accept that there is energy throughout the universe—dark energy, kinetic energy, solar energy, magnetic energy, gravity, and so forth. A chakra is an energy center in the body. It is generally envisioned as a wheel or swirl found in specific places along the spine (the word *chakra* is Sanskrit for "wheel"), spots where our nerves are bundled and our hormones secreted. They are connected by *prana*, which can be described as our life force or interpreted as our peripheral nervous system. It's really the same thing—the difference is in how you think about it and whether you believe we have the power to consciously influence it. Qi gong, tai chi, acupressure, acupuncture, EFT, and Reiki all work with *prana*, though they may call it different things (energy meridians, *nadis*, qi, etc.).

There are thought to be over a hundred chakras, but we tend to focus on just seven of them. In order for the body, mind, and spirit to be whole, each of these chakras needs to be open and balanced. A physical issue with a chakra can create an emotional or mental issue, and an emotional or mental issue that relates to a chakra can produce a physical response. Your body is not separate from your mind and spirit; all three are intertwined. A chakra can close for several reasons, including day-to-day life experiences, emotional trauma, cultural influences, lack of exercise, or lack of self-care. If you face a trauma, your chakra will respond to that experience by protecting itself. For example, if you lose a loved one, your closed heart chakra could cause you to develop asthma or bronchitis.

A chakra can also be overactive, so that it overpowers the other chakras. An overactive throat chakra can lead to gossip, deceit, or an inability to keep secrets. We've all experienced some serious oversharing on social media—blame an overactive throat chakra for that one.

It's all about balance. In the same way that each part of our body is a portion of a whole, each chakra responds to another, so that if one is out of balance, the others are all affected. A chakra should have energy flowing into it (so that, for instance, the heart chakra can accept love) and out of it (so that it can give love). A chakra that is balanced has an equal flow, back and forth, like the tides, and that flow resonates at a certain frequency. Each chakra has its own sound frequency as well as its own light frequency (color). We can use these sounds and colors to open or close each chakra as needed. When your chakras are in balance, you feel at ease within your whole self, as you are giving and receiving freely with the world.

THE SEVEN CHAKRAS

There are seven main chakras, and each one is connected to the physical, emotional, and spiritual body in its own way. Each one is associated with a color, an element, and a specific sound, which can be useful when chanting to open up the individual chakra.

muladhara

 This is the root chakra at the base of the spine, where the tailbone, bladder, and colon are located. This is the most instinctual of all chakras—our fight or flight response is seated here. It is our connection with the past, with our ancestral memories, and establishes our deepest connection with the earth. When this chakra is balanced, we feel utterly fearless and safe. Physical manifestations of imbalance can include problems with the legs, feet, and lower digestive system. Worries about our basic needs for survival food, shelter, money—may indicate that the root chakra is out of balance.

COLOR: red ✦ ESSENTIAL OILS: cedar, clove, myrrh ✦ SOUND: O

svadhisthana

 This is the sacral chakra, where the ovaries and testes are located. Unsurprisingly, this is the center of our creativity and sexuality. Our passions and pleasures, both physical and spiritual, stem from this place in the body. When this chakra is balanced, we are more fertile in every way—every idea, every song, every story grows from here. Physical

disruptions can include problems with fertility, kidney function, and hip and lower back pain. When the sacral chakra is overactive, we can be hedonistic and manic, and when it is blocked, we can have trouble finding pleasure in things we ordinarily enjoy.

COLOR: orange ✦ ESSENTIAL OILS: sandalwood, ylang-ylang ✦ SOUND: Oo

manipura

✦

Located at the solar plexus, near the adrenal glands and the endocrine system, Manipura is about personal power, our sense of self and our inner strength. This is where we find the source of our willpower, the drive that takes us from inertia to action. It is about confidence and choice. Someone with a balanced solar plexus chakra is assertive without being arrogant, in control without being afraid, and full of self-love. Someone whose solar plexus chakra is blocked might be hearing that negative inner voice, fearing rejection, or sitting quietly on the sidelines for fear of being wrong. On the other hand, an overactive solar plexus chakra causes emotional outbursts, stress, and a need to be the center of attention. Physical manifestations of imbalance include high blood pressure, chronic fatigue, and stomach ulcers.

COLOR: yellow ✦ ESSENTIAL OILS: chamomile, lemon ✦ SOUND: Ah

anahata

The heart chakra is, of course, seated at the heart, but also at the lungs. This is the center chakra, and it is responsible for maintaining the balance between the other six. And how else could we achieve that balance but with love? By love we mean romantic love, self-love, friendship, kindness, compassion, and respect. This is how we recognize that we are not alone, that we are part of a community, of a partnership, of a family. When we allow too much of this feeling, we can be needy or unwilling to set boundaries, even when we need to. And, of course, when we are closed off, we can feel abandoned, lonely, or jealous. Physically, a heart chakra that is out of balance can result in asthma and heart disease, as well as upper back and shoulder pain.

COLOR: green ✦ ESSENTIAL OILS: rose, bergamot ✦ SOUND: Ay

vishuddha

The throat chakra is located near the thyroid gland. If Manipura is about empowering ourselves, Vishuddha is about sharing our true selves. It is about speaking out, standing up for what we believe in, and presenting ourselves authentically to the world. When that is overdone, we can speak without compassion or interest in what others have to say. A balanced throat chakra means that we not only speak the truth, but we hear and accept it as well, which can often be the harder task. On the other hand, when the throat chakra is blocked, we are afraid to speak and share our true selves with the world for fear of rejection. This can manifest in thyroid issues, sore throat, neck pain, and mouth ulcers.

COLOR: light blue ✦ ESSENTIAL OILS: lavender, sage, neroli ✦ SOUND: Eee

ajna

✴

The third eye chakra is seated near the pituitary gland. We are beginning to get outside of the self now, as Ajna is about seeing things clearly. It's about observation and perception, but also wisdom. When our third eye chakra is balanced, we not only see what is happening around us, but also comprehend it, feeling it deeply, with compassion and understanding. As always, there can be too much of a good thing, result-ing in an overactive imagination, an inability to calm the mind, and a lack of focus. If we close the third eye too tightly, though, we cut our-selves off from the world around us, navel-gazing until we become paranoid and depressed. Physical symptoms of an unbalanced third eye chakra can include headaches, hearing loss, and blurred vision.

COLOR: indigo ✦ ESSENTIAL OILS: jasmine, vetiver, rosemary ✦ SOUND: Mmm

sahasrara

The crown chakra perches at the very top of the head, near the pineal gland and, of course, the brain. As we move to this chakra, we have left the self entirely—we are now focused not only on what is outside of ourselves, but what is *beyond* us. If magic is to be found in the chakras, it will be found here. There is no intellectual understanding in Sahasrara, but instead a mystical knowing, an intuitive understanding of our place in the universe, of our connection with all life. When the crown chakra is overactive, we tend to assume that we are more powerful/better than we really are, and we become judgmental and critical of others. When the crown chakra is closed, we feel isolated and lonely. We become uncertain, and we feel lost and depressed without a specific reason. Nightmares, migraines, and insomnia can all result from an imbalanced crown chakra.

COLOR: purple ✦ ESSENTIAL OILS: frankincense, olibanum ✦ SOUND: Ngngng

BALANCING YOUR CHAKRAS AS A WHOLE

Meditation is the most effective way to bring all your chakras into harmonious balance. Sit comfortably—there's no need for a perfectly straight back or lotus legs. Instead, sit in such a way that you're not in any pain or discomfort, but you're not likely to fall asleep, either. Remember that meditation is not about stopping all thought—that's an impossible goal. It is instead about allowing our thoughts to come and go, observing without engaging with them.

When you've achieved a state of open relaxation, begin to focus your attention on your root chakra. Visualize its color, and visualize its swirl as it allows energy to flow in and out evenly. Take a deep breath and chant "Ohhhhhh."

Continue in this manner up through each chakra, moving in order and taking the time to focus your attention on each one in turn, seeing its color in your mind and chanting its sound aloud. When you've finished, visualize yourself surrounded by a glow of white light. Repeat a mantra that feels appropriate to you in the moment; perhaps it is something like "I am at peace within myself," or "the Universe/a higher power/God is for me/us all." Breathe deeply and allow the energy to settle within you.

BALANCING THE INDIVIDUAL CHAKRAS

You can balance each individual chakra with a meditation practice. Make use of each chakra's suggested crystals (see page 22), along with its associated essential oils. You can either rest the crystal on the location of the specific chakra while you're lying down and meditating, or, if you prefer to sit up, simply hold it in your hand. Chant the sound associated with your chakra as many times as feels comfortable and right, or sit in silence, focusing your attention on that chakra.

But if meditation is simply beyond you, there are other ways to balance your chakras, specific to each of them:

MULADHARA ◆ Seek out the color red, particularly in your food. Let your bare feet feel the earth. Do something practical, like saving for retirement or paying a little extra toward your mortgage. Use the suggested essential oils in a footbath, or apply a warm cloth with a few drops of oil to the base of your spine.

SVADHISTHANA ✦ Engage in a little romance, even if that simply means watching *Bridget Jones's Diary* or reading a sweeping historical novel. Eat orange foods and indulge in any activity that brings you pleasure, particularly something creative. Drop some essential oils in a bath or shower, or use them to scent a candle.

MANIPURA ✦ Get some sunshine! Go to the beach, if it's the right season, or even just curl up inside near the window. Eat yellow foods, including lots of citrus, drink some chamomile tea, and give yourself a lot of self-care. Definitely knock off any negative self-talk!

ANAHATA ✦ Make time for those you love—call a friend you haven't talked to in a while, spend quality time with your partner or children, or take your parents out to dinner. For each act of love you give, you will receive that love back ten-fold. And while you're at it, eat lots of leafy greens, perhaps throwing in a beet or two.

VISHUDDHA ✦ Journal, blog, write some poetry, even sing! You may not be ready to share any of that with anyone else, but practice exercising your voice in whatever way you're comfortable. Seek out the color blue . . . there aren't many blue foods, obviously, but you could wear a blue shirt or simply choose to notice the blue you see in the world.

AJNA ✦ Make a point of listening closely when others are speaking. Read about what is going on in the world and ask questions. Ponder. Wear dark blue, and close your eyes so that you can reflect on what you have seen and heard.

SAHASRARA ✦ For this one, you really should meditate, if you can. If not, try prayer. Ask for guidance and be willing to listen for an answer. Look for purple around you. Imagine all the possibilities in the world, and even reflect on the *impossible.* Allow yourself to daydream.

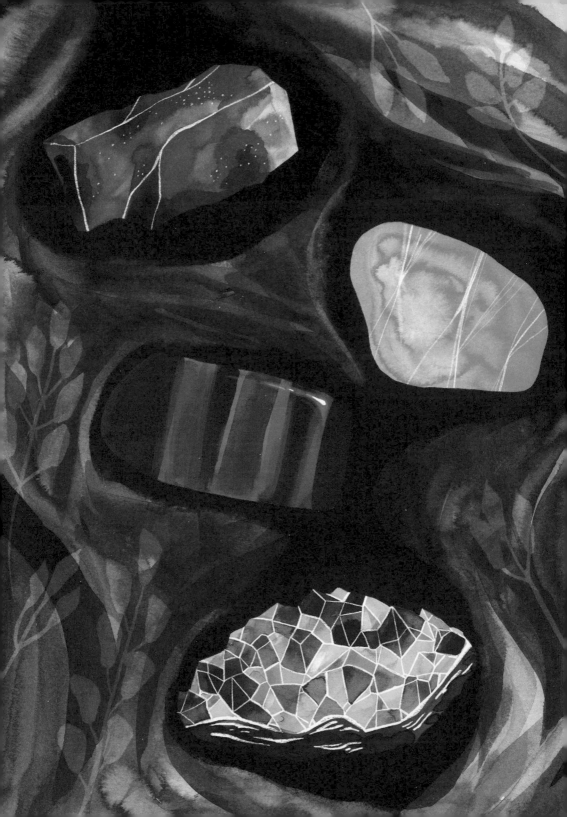

CRYSTALS

· ·

HONESTLY, PART OF THE REASON WE'RE DRAWN TO CRYSTAL healing is because it's so *pretty*—it just feels magical.

Whether it is truly magical is up for debate. There is evidence that crystal healing has been around for 6,000 years, dating back to Sumerians and ancient Egyptians. Today's crystal healing most often relates to the Buddhist and Hindu understanding of chakras. All of these different practices assign different properties to different stones—diamonds to draw out poison, garnet to keep nightmares away, jade for longevity, and so forth.

There hasn't been much in the way of real scientific research done on crystal healing, and what little there is shows nothing more than a placebo effect. But, worst-case scenario, crystal healing is utterly harmless, and according to its practitioners, it can achieve a staggeringly wide variety of results—everything from stimulating psychic abilities to aligning the spine and offsetting alcoholism.

Because there are so many stones with such varied uses, crystal healing can be a fairly complicated practice. The effect of each crystal changes not just with its type but also its shape and how it has been activated and cleansed. For instance, rose quartz will produce different results depending on whether it is shaped as a wand or left as a tumbled stone. For a professional session, a healer will interview you about your needs and concerns before having you lie on a mat or a massage table for the session. The healer will then place stones on or near your body as you remain still and try to achieve a state of comfort and relaxation—which isn't always easy with someone darting about putting rocks on and around you.

Most often, the placement relies on the chakras (see page 13):

MULADHARA, the root chakra, can be stimulated with red or black stones like obsidian, hematite, garnet, and smoky quartz.

SVADHISTHANA, the sacral chakra, responds to orange stones like citrine and carnelian.

MANIPURA, the solar plexus chakra, should be paired with yellow stones like yellow jasper and golden calcite.

ANAHATA, the heart chakra, traditionally responds to green stones like malachite and jade, but since our bodies are influenced by our minds and cultures, pink stones like rose quartz have gained in power and popularity for the healing of the heart.

VISHUDDHA, the throat chakra, is stimulated by blue stones, including aquamarine and turquoise.

AJNA, the chakra located right between your eyebrows, at your "third eye," is opened up by indigo stones like lapis lazuli and azurite.

SAHASRARA, the crown chakra at the top of your head, is paired with violet and white stones including amethysts and clear quartz.

After that, it's a matter of the healer's personal preference and interpretation of your needs. The healer will observe your reactions to each stone as it magnifies your positive energies and balances your negative energies. During or after a session you might experience some lethargy, a runny nose, and even some weeping as physical and emotional blockages are released.

Whether that's just a placebo effect, the power of your mind choosing to *believe* that it's working, or amethysts really taking your headache away . . . who knows? And if the headache is gone, does it matter?

THE MOST COMMON STONES AND THEIR USES

AMETHYST ✦ Develops intuition and spiritual awareness. Aids in meditation, calm, and tranquility. Relieves headaches.

AQUAMARINE ✦ Aids in expressing your personal truth. Reduces fear and tension.

AZURITE ✦ Helps find spiritual or psychic blocks that are causing physical blocks. Transforms fear into understanding. Good for arthritis and joint pain.

CALCITE ✦ An energy amplifier, it eases communication between the physical and spiritual world.

CARNELIAN ✦ Enhances creativity and sexuality, and helps with exploring past life experiences. Aids in digestion

CITRINE ✦ A stone of abundance, it invites success and money, and raises self-esteem. Good for the heart, kidneys, liver, and muscles.

CLEAR QUARTZ ✦ A stone of healing, it channels power and amplifies universal energy. This stone can be programmed to whatever use you require.

GARNET ✦ A stone of health and creativity, it stimulates your internal fire. Wards off cancer, good for skin elasticity, and also helps prevent nightmares.

HEMATITE ✦ A stone of protection and grounding, it closes your aura to keep out negative energy. Provides support for astral projection.

JADE ✦ Will inspire you to ambition and keep you working toward your objective. Good for longevity.

LAPIS LAZULI ✦ A stone of focus that helps amplify thought, aids in meditation, and releases you from melancholy. Good for sore throats and fever.

MALACHITE ✦ Releases stored emotions, allows you to look inward. Useful in alleviating mental illness.

MOONSTONE ✦ Soothes the emotions as well as the digestive system. Encourages peace and harmony within.

OBSIDIAN ✦ A stone of protection, particularly from spiritual forces. It will help you to understand and face your deepest fears. Helps with bacterial and viral invasions.

OPAL ✦ Stone of amplification, enhances mystical experiences and creativity. Balances mood swings.

PYRITE ✦ A stone of defense and protection, it symbolizes the sun and cleanses the blood.

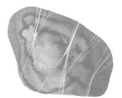

ROSE QUARTZ ✦ A stone of love—not just romantic love, but familial and brotherly love as well. Nurturing and comforting, this stone dissipates anger.

SMOKY QUARTZ ✦ A stone of protection, it stimulates your survival instincts. Enhances focus and fertility.

TIGER'S EYE ✦ A stone of stability, it heightens personal power and integrity.

TURQUOISE ✦ A stone of healing, it guards against disease and environmental pollutants.

YELLOW JASPER ✦ Stimulates the pancreas and the endocrine system. Helps align the energy meridians.

HOW TO CHOOSE AND ACTIVATE YOUR CRYSTAL

The first step is to determine your needs at the moment. Are you addressing a physical ailment or a spiritual one? Are you going to attempt astral projection or perhaps a spell? Sometimes you might find yourself drawn to a particular stone, so that the stone chooses you, rather than the other way around. Go to a holistic shop and see what calls to you.

If you're not sure what stone you need, try quartz. It's the salt in the spice cabinet of crystals.

Once you've chosen the type of stone you want to work with, you need to select its shape:

CHUNK ✦ This is a crystal without noticeable facets—turquoise often comes in this form, as does pyrite. While geodes have some facets, they are considered chunk crystals as well. These are often placed around the living space or work environment to cleanse the atmosphere.

CUT ✦ This is when a crystal or gem has been shaped to enhance sparkle and capture light, which amplifies the crystal's energies.

TUMBLED ✦ These are the stones you'll find in bins at a science or mystical shop. They are smooth, shiny, and comforting to hold.

WAND ✦ This type of crystal, rough at one end and pointed at the other, is frequently used in jewelry, but a healer may also use it to direct energies in a more pronounced and targeted way.

Once you've chosen a stone, you'll want to clear it. Your stone didn't come to you straight from the earth—it was found by others, packaged by others, and handled by others, so their energies have penetrated it. There are several ways to purify your crystal: soaking it in salt water or holding it under running water (preferably a stream, but rain or even your faucet will do in a pinch) are the simplest ways, but if your stone is a bit too delicate for that, you can let it rest with carnelian or clear quartz, which have cleansing properties; do a little smudging (see page 60); or let the sun or moon work their magic by "washing" the stones in their light.

Once the stone is cleared, it can be activated. While each stone always carries its special properties within itself, you can enhance a stone's power by programming it with your specific needs and intentions. Clear quartz in particular can become whatever you want it to be and do whatever you require it to do.

Activating your crystal can take any form you desire. This can be as simple as holding the crystal in your hand and setting an intention. You can invoke a higher power, or you can really set the stage for your healing process by performing a ritual.

Stand in pure light, either sunlight or moonlight, depending on your needs, cupping the crystal so that the light shines on it. Speak aloud a phrase of your choosing, invoking love and light in a way that speaks to you. If you are using your crystal for a specific purpose, name that purpose, and focus your intention into the stone. Hold the crystal to your heart and bow your head, giving thanks to the energy within the stone, or to a higher power—whichever feels right to you.

Once you've activated your stone, you can use some small-gauge wire and a chain to make it into a necklace for a lovely piece of supportive jewelry. You can simply carry it around in your pocket, put it into a gris-gris bag or incorporate it into your spellwork (see pages 61 and 77), or place it around your home to ward and protect you.

Ketheric Template Aura
Celestial Aura
Etheric Template Aura
Astral Aura
Mental Aura
Emotional Aura
Etheric Aura

AURAS

· ·

WE'VE ALL HAD THAT MOMENT WHEN WE FEEL UNCOMFORTABLY close to someone in an elevator or on the street, as if they had touched us unexpectedly, even if they didn't. We back away as much as we can. That sense of discomfort, of invasion, happens to everyone. It also works the other way—sometimes the act of just being near someone we love, or whose energy inspires us, can be comforting and provide a physical sensation of warmth and ease. We can call that invisible something around us our "space," our "bubble," our "energy field," but the spiritual term for it is our *aura*.

All living things are surrounded by an aura. A typical aura spreads three feet away from the body, though the actual size depends on the person. Try rubbing your palms together furiously, generating heat. Then stop and let them drift slowly apart, paying attention to the energy you feel between them, the vibrations, the trembling, and the remaining heat. That is your own aura.

The energy that flows through the body, concentrated in the chakras, spills beyond the skin to interact with the world outside. In that way, whatever we're feeling inside is reflected outside. If we are out of balance, someone who can read auras can see that. But these imbalances make themselves clear in other ways, too. Every time we interpret someone's behavior, we read their internal imbalance: "My husband snapped at me. I know he's stressed out at work." "My friend is so tired all the time. I know she's not paying enough attention to self-care." We often don't even need any supporting actions to understand these things—we can tell through simple body language or facial expressions or even some unnameable sense. It's with that unnameable sense that reading auras comes in.

An aura has seven layers called the subtle bodies, and these layers can fluctuate in visibility and size depending on the person's internal state. So someone's aura does not always look the same and is not always the same color. Everything depends on which layer is dominant at a specific moment.

ETHERIC AURA ✦ This layer lies closest to the physical body. At its resting state it extends only one to two inches outside the skin. It contains information about a person's physical well-being. This is what can be seen through electromagnetic or Kirlian photography. Its color typically varies between blue, when the person is more sedentary and tends to be emotional, and gray, when the person is more active.

EMOTIONAL AURA ✦ This subtle body extends three inches from the body and pertains to a person's emotional state. The emotional aura can be any color and may contain blotches signifying different emotions. If the person's emotional state is confused or conflicted, the aura will appear muddied.

MENTAL AURA ✦ This aura extends eight inches from the body. If a person is deep in thought, this layer will appear bright yellow with colors sparking depending on which emotions are associated with the thoughts.

ASTRAL AURA ✦ The first three aural layers are grounded in the self. Starting with this layer, things get a little wild. The astral aura is closely tied with the emotional aura, but it reflects the higher self or the best version of ourselves. When we are in love—romantic or platonic—it glows pink. This layer is the bridge to astral projection, and it extends about a foot away from the body.

ETHERIC TEMPLATE AURA ✦ This aura extends about two feet from the body, and it can be very difficult to see—and to understand. The etheric template aura is essentially a blueprint for all physical life. It appears as a dark blue.

CELESTIAL AURA ◆ This subtle body extends about two and a half feet from the body. Its colors tend to be shimmering, soft pastels, and the layer represents our communication with the Divine. Emotions of ecstatic love tap into this layer, as love is our strongest connection with the spiritual realm.

KETHERIC TEMPLATE AURA ◆ This aura extends approximately three feet from the body and shines like a structured web of gold. If the celestial aura relates to our emotional connection with the Divine, the ketheric template aura is tied in with our mental and spiritual knowing. Our intuition resides here.

Though we are all able to sense auras, we are not all able to sense every layer, at least not individually—only extremely experienced practitioners can do that. Once we've taught ourselves to actually see the auras, not simply sense them, we may still have a hard time interpreting them because the layers lie on top of one another, so that what we are looking at is a blend of all the layers. This still gives us a lot of information and allows us to interpret what we see. An aura will rarely be just one color, but frequently one specific color tends to dominate. If that color is clear and bright, the aura is considered healthy, but if it is muddied, the person may be experiencing some emotional issues.

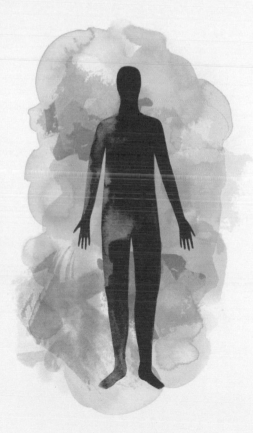

COMMON AURAL COLORS AND THEIR MEANINGS

A red aura can be difficult to interpret, as it can indicate either positive or negative energies. Use your own emotional response to the person's aura to help you figure that out. Red can mean healthy pride and sense of self-worth, or it can indicate anger and anxiety. From a physical standpoint, a red aura provides a picture of the heart and blood circulation.

DARK RED: Usually indicates someone who is centered and grounded, with a strong sense of self-preservation.

MUDDY RED: Indicates anger.

BRIGHT RED: Passionate, competitive, sensual, and energetic.

PINK: Artistic and loving. If this is not the person's usual aural color, it may have turned pink because they have recently fallen in love or are feeling love more profoundly at that moment. It may also indicate that the person possesses psychic abilities.

MUDDY PINK: Indicates deceit and emotional immaturity—which is frequently the cause of deceit.

orange

An orange aura generally means that the person is healthy and full of vitality and energy. It also provides an understanding of what is going on with the person's reproductive system.

> **RED ORANGE:** Indicates confidence.
>
> **YELLOW ORANGE:** This person is creative, intelligent, and a perfectionist.
>
> **MUDDY ORANGE:** This person is feeling laziness or a lack of ambition. They may also be emotionally clogged and unable move forward.

yellow

This person is optimistic and full of life and fun, though a yellow aura may also indicate that the person's liver or spleen is malfunctioning.

> **PASTEL YELLOW:** Optimism and spiritual awareness.
>
> **BRIGHT YELLOW:** Struggle for personal power.
>
> **MUDDY YELLOW:** Indicative of fatigue, from trying to do too much all at once.

green

Many teachers and healers have green auras, as do those who work with the natural world. It is the color of love and healing. Someone with a green aura works to help the world in whatever way they can. A green aura also provides information on the health of the heart and the lungs.

> **YELLOW GREEN:** Excellent communicator.
>
> **BRIGHT GREEN:** Natural healer.
>
> **MUDDY GREEN:** Jealousy, insecurity. This person has trouble taking responsibility for their actions.

blue

People with blue auras are calm and compassionate, sensitive and intuitive. A blue aura may also tell you something about the state of the thyroid.

TURQUOISE: Powerful healer, particularly in the realm of emotional and
mental health.

LIGHT BLUE: Truthful and peaceful.

BRIGHT BLUE: A spiritual intuitive. May be able to read other's thoughts
or futures.

MUDDY BLUE: Deceitful, though not out of malice, but instead out of fear.

purple

Those with purple auras are deeply spiritual and possess extraordinary gifts, though a purple aura may also indicate that something is going on with the nervous system.

INDIGO: A daydreamer, but in the best possible way. This person can make
the world the way they wish it to be.

VIOLET: Psychically powerful and wise.

LAVENDER: Imaginative and creative.

MUDDY VIOLET: This person's psychic gifts are being blocked by some
internal force.

silver

A silver aura is indicative of abundance, either spiritually or monetarily. On the other hand, a gray aura indicates that the person is filled with fear to the point of suffering physically.

gold

Someone with a gold aura is in direct communication with the Divine. Many of our great spiritual leaders, like Gandhi and Martin Luther King Jr., would have gold auras.

black

If someone's aura is black, they are pulling all energy toward themself, like a black hole. These individuals are psychically or physically wounded and trying to heal themselves, however ineffectively.

white

White indicates newness and purity. Celestial beings are said to have white auras. Someone who is enlightened may have a white aura, though children often have white auras as well.

HOW TO SEE AURAS

First, get comfortable *sensing* auras. We all do this instinctively, so it's just a matter of consciously paying more attention. Take a person on the train or sitting near you in the park, and observe them. What is your gut reaction? Use all of your senses, if you can—what do they look like, sound like, smell like? What is your emotional response? Go ahead and assign that person a color. Try not to pin down any meaning of the color in your mind first. Just go with your instincts and intuition.

Next, try utilizing your peripheral vision. Out of the sides of our eyes we often half-see objects and colors that aren't really there—or at least aren't usually visible. Our peripheral vision provides us with far more information than we normally allow ourselves access to. If you look at the person out of the corner of your eye, do you sense a color? You can develop this peripheral vision through practice.

To take a more intentional approach, ask the person to stand in front of a white wall, and sway gently from side to side. Use a soft focus to look at them. Allow your eyes to blur. Don't strain or squint—this isn't something that requires good eyesight, as it isn't really about seeing at all. Any colors that you see in the space the person just occupied will indicate their aura.

HOW TO CLEANSE YOUR AURA

Cleansing your aura is not that different from balancing the chakras. The most profound difference is really that it needs to happen more often, because auras are more easily and frequently affected by the outside world than chakras. Just brushing up against a negative aura can introduce negativity into our own auras. Unexplained mood swings or a good time turning instantly bad can be the result of the impact of someone else's aura on your own.

Cleanse your aura by going through the chakra-cleansing ritual (see page 17), and then work to strengthen that aura from further invasion. During meditation, visualize a psychic wall of protection around your energy field, a wall that is permeable only to what you wish to allow inside. It can close out anger, block those who drain your energy, and welcome in love and positivity.

There are also cords that bind us to everyone around us—thick, unbreakable cords between those we love the most and threads connecting strangers to one another. Those threads can always grow back, but sometimes you need the space to heal yourself. Visualize breaking those threads and allowing the thick, unbreakable cords to go slack—still connected, but no longer pulling at you. If there is a cord that needs to be broken or weakened—say, if a friendship has become toxic—visualize that as well.

If your aura feels too diffuse—if you are feeling that you are spread too thin—visualize your aura contracting. Rein it in, keeping your energies close to your heart.

If meditation and visualization are hard for you, you're not alone! There are also more physical, tangible ways to cleanse your aura. Water is an excellent way to rinse your aura, particularly moving water like a stream, a waterfall, or the ocean. If that isn't available to you, try taking a saltwater bath. Crystals can be extremely helpful, as can certain herbal remedies.

PART 2

MAGIC FOR THE WEEKEND WICCAN

Herbs for healing, herbs for spells . . .
dance at dawn to welcome Beltane, and
revel in your inner witch.

HEALING with HERBS

• •

THERE'S SOMETHING DELIGHTFUL ABOUT THE PHRASE *HERBAL tinctures. Elixir,* too, has a tantalizingly old-fashioned magic to it. For better or worse, though, herbal remedies are not magical at all. Take aspirin: it was hailed as wonder drug in the early 1900s . . . but people had been chewing willow bark for centuries and achieving the same result. Both contain salicylic acid, the active ingredient in aspirin that provides pain relief. We switched to swallowing aspirin instead of drinking willow bark tea because we were able to ingest a higher concentration of the salicylic acid all at once. Also (bonus!) we didn't have to taste willow bark.

These days, pharmaceuticals are viewed with a little more caution and a little less enthusiasm. We've all dealt with our share of side effects, price-gouging, and concerns about addiction and overdose. The truth is that aspirin, ibuprofen, or naproxen is going to be far more effective than turmeric, stinging nettle, or willow bark. You'd need to eat *a lot* of turmeric to get the same level of pain relief that naproxen can give you. On the other hand, turmeric isn't going to make your stomach bleed or cause kidney or liver problems, while naproxen might. If you've got a migraine or a slipped disc in your back, take the naproxen. If you've got a mild headache or some sore muscles, maybe consider flavoring your dinner with a lot of turmeric.

Herbs can help with a wide range of issues, from upset stomach to cramps to depression to allergy relief. You're likely already familiar with (and use) various healing plants like echinacea, ginger, kava, and chamomile. But have you considered the benefits of catnip, milk thistle, and horse chestnut?

The *easiest* thing to do is to buy some supplements—but it may not be the *best* thing to do. It is also possible to do yourself harm with herbal remedies—they can interact with over-the-counter or prescription medications you may be on, and if you take more than the recommended dosage, you might start having trouble with your liver or blood pressure. And let's be smart here—don't take *anything* while pregnant without consulting with your doctor first.

If you use herbal remedies in tea or tincture form, you're much less likely to take too much. It's also just more *fun*—tending a healing garden, hanging herbs to dry, and making teas, tinctures, compresses, and pastes is nothing short of delightful. The hedge witches of old knew how to find and use every possible plant for every possible remedy—skills that were so impressive that they seemed like magic.

COMMON HERBS AND THEIR USES

ashwagandha

✳

The name translates to "smell of horse." This herb is hard to find fresh, but powders, pills, teas, and extracts are available.

BENEFITS: Increases energy, boosts the immune system, anti-inflammatory, reduces anxiety.

SUGGESTED USE: Stir ¼-½ tsp. powder into warm milk and honey before bed.

CONCERNS: May increase thyroid hormone levels and lower blood sugar.

black cohosh

✳

This member of the buttercup family could be grown in a garden. Dried roots, capsules, teas, and extracts are also available.

BENEFITS: Relieves menstrual cramps and arthritic pain. Eases symptoms of menopause.

SUGGESTED USE: Drink as a tea or mix with honey as a syrup.

CONCERNS: May cause upset stomach, so consider taking with food.

calendula
✴

Also known as marigold, this herb could be grown in a garden, but is also available as teas, oils, and creams. Useful for dyeing and food coloring as well.

BENEFITS: Helps heal cuts. Good for diaper rash or other skin irritations. Calms an upset stomach.

SUGGESTED USE: Steep petals in just below boiling water for ten minutes, then drink as a tea. Add dried flowers to coconut, almond, or olive oil as a salve.

CONCERNS: None known.

catnip
✴

It's not just for cats! Catnip is easily grown and also available as a capsule, tea, extract, and essential oil. It is also handy as an insect repellent.

BENEFITS: Anti-inflammatory. Good for insomnia, upset stomach, menstrual cramps, headache, and treating the common cold.

SUGGESTED USES: Steep for tea, sprinkle essential oil into the bath or rub it on the temples, use in cooking (it's a member of the mint family, so its flavor is better than some).

CONCERNS: None known.

cranberry
✴

Easily obtained fresh or frozen and also available in pill form, this herb is a great source of vitamin C, fiber, and vitamin E.

BENEFITS: Most frequently used to treat and prevent urinary tract infections. Also shown to reduce risk of cardiovascular disease, slow tumor progression in cancer, and help prevent gum disease.

SUGGESTED USES: Because they're so tart, cranberries often come with a *lot* of sugar. Try to buy reduced-sugar dried cranberries and stay away from most cranberry juices. If you can manage it, drink the unsweetened juice to relieve a UTI, and certainly try making your own cranberry sauce at Thanksgiving.

CONCERNS: None known.

dittany
✳

This is one of those herbs with a long history. It is also known as "burning bush." Easily grown, it is hard to find in dried or tea form.

BENEFITS: Antibacterial, antifungal, and antimicrobial. Good for the skin and the intestines, and is thought to be an aphrodisiac.

SUGGESTED USES: Steep in hot water for tea, but use sparingly. Use as an antibacterial balm or poultice.

CONCERNS: If you've put some on your skin, stay out of the sun, as it can increase the risk of sunburn.

elderberry
✳

This herb has been used to battle a flu epidemic in Panama as recently as 1995. It can be grown, but is also available as a pill or an extract. For your personal garden, look specifically for *Sambucus nigra*, as other elderberry varieties can be toxic.

BENEFITS: Boosts the immune system, treats sinus infections, lowers blood sugar, acts as a diuretic and a laxative, good for skin health and allergies.

SUGGESTED USES: They're delicious! Can be made into a syrup, jams, or jellies—even wine.

CONCERNS: Don't pick and use wild elderberry unless you're absolutely certain the plant is *Sambucus nigra*. Always cook the berries to remove any toxicity.

feverfew

This is another herb with a long history. Easily grown and available dried, it is most frequently found in capsule form.

BENEFITS: For centuries, it was used to relieve fever, to assist with childbirth, and for fertility. Now it is most frequently used to prevent migraines. It can also help with tinnitus, nausea, dizziness, asthma, and allergies.

SUGGESTED USES: It doesn't taste good, so not recommended even as a tea. Instead, make a tincture or purchase capsules.

CONCERNS: If you do drink it, feverfew can cause irritation in the mouth. If taken in large quantities on a regular basis, stopping can cause withdrawal symptoms, so use only as needed. May cause the uterus to contract, so don't take while pregnant.

horse chestnut

This is not the kind of chestnut you'd want to roast on a fire, but it is still useful. It is not recommended for personal processing, as the seed contains esculin, a poisonous substance. Purchase an extract or pill instead.

BENEFITS: Shown to be extremely effective against varicose veins. Also good
for hemorrhoids and frostbite.

SUGGESTED USES: 300 milligrams of horse chestnut seed extract twice daily.

CONCERNS: Don't consume raw horse chestnut seeds, bark, or leaves.

lemon balm

This member of the mint family has a distinct lemony scent. It is also known as
"melissa." It is easily grown, but also available in tea, extract, and essential oil forms.

BENEFITS: Calms anxiety, encourages restful sleep. Good for the skin, improves
mood and mental clarity.

SUGGESTED USES: Steep fresh or dried to make tea, use in cooking, use to
flavor honey or vinegar, use in a hot bath.

CONCERNS: None known.

marshmallow

Sadly, these are not the things we put in hot chocolate. The root is available
dried, as well as in powder, extract, capsule, and tea form.

BENEFITS: Aids with dry cough, represses inflammation in the lining of the
stomach, good for chilblains and sunburn.

SUGGESTED USES: Drink as a tea, add to a base oil for a salve.

CONCERNS: May cause low blood sugar.

milk thistle
✳

This herb is easily grown, as it's pretty much a weed. It's available as an extract, pill, or tea.

> **BENEFITS:** Milk thistle can protect your liver from toxins—say, for instance, alcohol. It can even be used to treat cirrhosis and jaundice and helps with environmental toxin damage.
> **SUGGESTED USES:** Steep in hot water or make a tincture. Not recommended for use in cooking.
> **CONCERNS:** May cause diarrhea.

mullein
✳

This is the clear quartz of herbal healing. It is easily found and grown and available both dried and in capsule form.

BENEFITS: Known particularly for respiratory relief, including cough, bronchitis, asthma, and pneumonia, it's also good for earache, fever, sore throat, migraine, and to heal the skin.

SUGGESTED USES: Apply a tincture to relieve ear infection, drink as a tea, use as a salve to heal wounds and bruises.

CONCERNS: None known.

plantain leaf

Pretty hip these days, as herbal remedies go, plantain leaf is easily grown and available dried or in capsule form.

BENEFITS: Great for the skin, particularly in relieving insect bites, poison ivy, and sunburn. Lowers cholesterol, helps clear up bladder infections, relieves constipation or diarrhea.

SUGGESTED USES: Make poultice with clay and water or make a salve with a base oil. Infuse vinegar to spray on the skin to provide pain relief. Drink as a tea.

CONCERNS: None known.

rue

This herb is also known as "herb of grace." Easily grown, it is also available dried, in capsule form, or as an essential oil.

BENEFITS: Used to promote menstruation, it provides a sense of calm and well-being and is good for relieving gas, mucus, and arthritis.

SUGGESTED USES: As an oil or poultice it can relieve croup or chest congestion. Drink as a tea to ease anxiety.

CONCERNS: This one is serious—it can cause a miscarriage. Use in small amounts, regardless of whether or not you're pregnant.

valerian

This is an attractive addition to any garden, with a pleasing scent, but it is the root which holds the good stuff and that does *not* smell good. Easily grown, this herb is also available in tea, capsule, and extract forms.

> **BENEFITS:** Valerian is very effective against insomnia. It also calms anxiety and depression, and helps with ADHD and headache.
>
> **SUGGESTED USES:** Drink a tea made from the leaves for a mild sedative, or steep the roots for something stronger. Add a tincture to a bath for a gentler, child-friendly alternative.
>
> **CONCERNS:** None known, but obviously don't operate heavy machinery.

vervain

Usually blue vervain is used, but other types seem to work just as well. Easily grown, vervain is also available dried or as an extract.

BENEFITS: Helps with anxiety and sleeplessness. Also provides pain relief, eases tense muscles, and promotes an overall sense of well-being.

SUGGESTED USES: Steep in hot water as a tea. Not recommended in cooking, though it smells nice, so add a little to a bath.

CONCERNS: May cause nausea.

yarrow
✳

This member of the sunflower family is easily grown—and quite lovely—and available dried or as an essential oil.

BENEFITS: Relieves fever, as well as cold and flu symptoms. Relieves cramps, provides a sense of calm and relaxation, and aids in restful sleep. Suppresses the urge to urinate (say, during a UTI). Use topically for a rash or small cuts.

SUGGESTED USES: Drink as a tea in the evening to induce sleepiness or relieve cold and flu symptoms, or make into a salve for external use.

CONCERNS: None known.

HOW TO MAKE A TINCTURE

Making a tincture involves steeping the herb or root in alcohol, extracting its oils, minerals, alkaloids, and glycosides so that it is in its purest form. You can use vegetable glycerin or apple cider vinegar instead, particularly in tinctures intended for children, but they aren't quite as effective at pulling out the good stuff.

You'll need strong alcohol, at least 80 proof. Everclear works well, as does vodka or brandy. You'll also need a pint jar to fill with the herb or plant you want—any of the herbs listed above will work here. Chop the herb up a bit or bash it around with a mortar and pestle to help it break down. You'll want the jar to be full, but not pack your herbs in too tightly. Then fill the jar completely with the alcohol. (If you're using dried herbs or roots, you need only put in enough to reach halfway, and then add the alcohol up to the top.)

Seal the jar tightly. Label and date it, and let it rest in a cool, dark place. For the first week, shake it once a day, then let it rest for five more weeks.

At the end of the resting period, use a layer of muslin or cheesecloth held tightly over the jar to strain out the liquid. Decant the tincture into one of those small, dark glass bottles, preferably one with a dropper, and keep it stored away from direct sunlight. It should last for five to ten years.

HOW TO MAKE HERBAL OIL

It's more trouble than it's worth to make your own essential oils. A true essential oil is extracted by boiling the herb in question and skimming the oil off the top—that's a task best left to the professionals.

But you can make your own herbal oil. It may not be quite as distilled, but it can still be effective, and it's a great way to preserve herbs for use long into the winter. The nice thing about creating your own oils is that you can use any combination of herbs that you desire. You might mix calendula, catnip, lemon balm, marshmallow, mullein, plantain leaf, and yarrow for an oil that is particularly effective for skin care, or lavender, vervain, lemon balm, and yarrow for a soothing oil to rub on the temples.

Chop or bruise your chosen herbs and place them in a jar. Fill the jar with the carrier oil of your choice (olive or almond oil works well), covering the herbs by one inch, and leaving one inch of space at the top. Close the jar tightly, and allow it to sit in as much sunshine as possible for a month.

Strain the oil through a cheesecloth on an as-needed basis, leaving the rest to continue steeping.

HOW TO MAKE A POULTICE

A poultice is a soft, moist mass of herbs, cloth, and other ingredients, and it's an excellent tool for treating topical infirmities. A hot poultice is excellent for drawing out infection, as with bee stings or draining abscesses, while a cold poultice will help reduce inflammation.

Gather the herbs you want to use, either fresh or dried. If they're fresh, you may want to mash the herbs up in a mortar and pestle (the traditional way) or blitz them through a food processor (the modern way). Even if you're planning on making a cold poultice, add a couple of tablespoons of hot water to your herbs to awaken them, before letting them cool. You can add medicinal clay powder, Epsom salts, or baking soda and combine with water until the mixture becomes a thick paste.

For ailments like congestion or insect bites, you can place the poultice directly on the skin, making sure, of course, that it isn't too hot. To treat a burn or something that could easily become infected, place a clean cotton cloth between the skin and the poultice.

PLANT-BASED MAGIC

· ·

IT'S A SHORT LEAP FROM PRACTICING HERBAL HEALING TO practicing herbal magic. If you think about it, we make potions all the time. A calming DIY face mask? That's a potion. Those amazing bath bombs at LUSH? Totally potions. It may not seem like magic because we aren't talking "double, double toil and trouble; fire burn, and cauldron bubble" here—but in fact, ingredients like "eye of newt" and "toe of frog" were actually just folk names. Eye of newt is another term for mustard seed, and frog's feet were buttercups. It's been argued that these folk names were really code names that practicing witches used to keep their potion recipes secret, while having a good laugh about some poor fool scampering off to risk his life for a wolf's claw when all he really needed was some moss.

So what is all this mustard seed and moss supposed to do? Generally speaking, as with so much else in this book, it's about *energy*. Like chakras and crystals (see pages 11 and 21), herbal magic is frequently about bringing your body, mind, and spirit into balance. You will use the herbs in the same way you do crystals and chakras—by harnessing your *prana*, your energy, and directing it in a positive, loving way.

That's not to say herbs can't be used in spells! There are love spells, spells for protection, money spells, luck spells, and spells for happiness. There are also plants that are sometimes used for darker magic, as well—yew can be used to invite death, and parsley can bring bad luck. (For whatever reason, parsley was thought to be *really evil*.) But it's about intention. Putting a little parsley in a dinner you're making for a friend is not going to harm them—unless you want it to. And at that point, who is to say that it's the parsley that's at fault? It's really about the negative energy you're bringing to the friendship (something that clearly needs to be addressed!).

The same is true for light magic—it is always about intention. If you cook a dish of stewed tomatoes with dill, basil, and cinnamon, and you focus your energy on inviting abundance, you might find yourself catching a financial windfall. (Mind you, your dinner might taste a little strange.) And of course it's not just about cooking. Botanomancy, the practice of divination through herbs, involves burning specific plants or trees and reading messages in the ashes or watching the way the smoke moves. Gathering vervain under a new moon and placing it under your pillow will draw the object of your affections to you as you sleep. Holly placed under the pillow will induce prophetic dreams.

Most plant-based magic is less about casting spells than it is about using plants with specific magical properties in intentional ways. Placing specific plants around the home, consuming them (if they are safe), burning them, carrying them around the neck in a small bag—these are all the most common and effective ways of bringing herb witchery into your life.

COMMON PLANTS AND THEIR USES IN MAGIC

BELLADONNA, AKA "DEADLY NIGHTSHADE" ◆ Poisonous, so do not ingest. Used for flight (on a broom and for astral projection), for youth and beauty spells, and to summon the dead.

BETONY ◆ For purification and protection. Prevents nightmares.

CARAWAY ◆ Good for love spells, and as an aphrodisiac.

CINQUEFOIL ◆ Prosperity, purification, and protection.

CLOVER ◆ Cures madness, also useful in youth and beauty rituals.

COWSLIP ◆ Invites those who have passed to visit in dreams.

DRAGON'S BLOOD ◆ Cures impotency, good for love spells.

ELECAMPANE ◆ Aids in raising spirits.

EYEBRIGHT ◆ Make a tincture and anoint your eyelids to induce visions.

FRANKINCENSE ◆ Powerful aid to meditation.

GARLIC ◆ Protection, healing, courage, and, of course, exorcism.

HAWTHORN ◆ Protects against evil spirits, good for marital happiness.

HELLEBORE ◆ Can make you invisible. Useful in exorcisms.

HENBANE ◆ Aids in flight (on a broom, but also astral projection). Poisonous, so do not ingest.

HOLLY ◆ Powerful protection against evil. Enhances masculinity. Invites prophetic dreams.

HONEYSUCKLE ◆ Useful for prosperity and love charms.

HYSSOP ◆ Purifies. Useful in preparation for astral projection and for banishing evil spirits.

JUNIPER ◆ Protects against accidents and theft.

LAVENDER ◆ Provides clarity of thought, aids in having visions. Good for peace and protection.

LEMON BALM ◆ Aphrodisiac, also soothes a broken heart.

MANDRAKE ◆ Powerful protective charm. Increases strength and courage, as well as virility and fertility.

MARIGOLD ◆ Useful in prophesying. Helps you see magical creatures. Use when conducting business or legal affairs.

MARJORAM ◆ Helps overcome grief.

MISTLETOE ◆ Mainly used in love spells and to aid in conception, also provides protection.

MUGWORT ✦ The go-to herb for witchery. Aids in astral projection, enhances psychic abilities, prevents fatigue.

MYRTLE ✦ Long history of use in love spells.

PIMPERNEL ✦ Helps detect lies and deceit.

ROSEMARY ✦ The phrase to keep in mind is "rosemary for remembrance." Improves memory and mental function, useful in youth spells.

SAGE ✦ Good for fertility and wisdom. Also aids in health and longevity.

ST. JOHN'S WORT ✦ Increases courage and willpower, good for banishing evil spirits.

THYME ✦ Renews energy, purifies the spirit.

VERVAIN ✦ Cleanses ritual spaces. Good for prosperity and creativity.

WORMWOOD ✦ Releases the wandering dead so they may rest. Useful in divination.

YARROW ✦ Enhances perception and psychic abilities.

HOW TO MAKE A SMUDGE STICK

A smudge stick is a small bundle of plants that will be lit on fire to release their properties into the air. Normally smudge sticks are used to dissipate negative energy in a space, so you can make a cleansing stick out of vervain, thyme, hyssop, and betony or a protective stick with some combination of St. John's wort, mandrake, hawthorn, garlic, and cinquefoil. You can also invite love into your life with a smudge stick of myrtle, mistletoe, honeysuckle, dragon's blood, and caraway. Or you can combine sage for wisdom, rosemary for clarity, and marigold in order to get your mental state clear and ready for business.

You can use fresh or dried plants for your smudge stick. Lay your choices together in a bundle—you'll want to create a stick that is at least five inches long, so that you can hold it comfortably while it burns. Use a cotton string to wrap the bundle into a firm stick, winding your way up and down the length of the stems. Go ahead and wrap tightly. If you've used fresh plants, hang them upside down to dry for a week before burning.

Light the tip of your smudge stick with a candle. Once it has a steady flame, blow it out so that the smudge stick is just smoldering, with smoke rising from the glowing tip. Fan the smoke over your head or around the room, using your hands to disperse it. To extinguish your smudge stick, smother the flame—try to avoid using water, as this will mean you can't reuse the stick.

HOW TO MAKE A GRIS-GRIS

Gris-gris go by any number of names, including sachets, charm bags, spell bags, and hex bags. They are small enough to carry with you, or they can be placed under your pillow, left in your car, or given as gifts.

Begin by choosing the fabric for your bag. Leather, velvet, and felt are common options, and they all have different connotations. Velvet might bring to mind wealth or romance, while leather might invoke strength or protection. Felt is the most commonly used, just because of its simplicity.

The color of your fabric is also important, for similar reasons. Look back to the colors of the chakras (see page 13) for guidance here.

To create your bag, cut two two- or three-inch squares of material and sew them together, leaving one side open. As you sew, focus your energy on what your gris-gris will hold and bring to you. Turn it inside out and fill the bag with the herbs of your choice, as well as any stones, crystals, runes, affirmations, or images that fit your purpose.

Sew the opening of your bag closed, and if desired, stitch on a ribbon so that you can wear it around your neck.

Here are a few ideas to consider:

FOR COURAGE: St. John's wort, garlic, tiger's-eye, and aquamarine in a yellow bag.

FOR ABUNDANCE: Marigold, cinquefoil, honeysuckle, jade, and citrine in a red bag.

FOR LOVE: Myrtle, mistletoe, honeysuckle, lemon balm, dragon's blood, caraway, rose quartz, and carnelian in a pink or green bag.

FOR MAGIC: Yarrow, wormwood, mugwort, lavender, henbane, hellebore, opal, lapis lazuli, and calcite in a purple bag.

61

PAGAN HOLIDAYS

. . . .

WE SEE WORDS LIKE *BELTANE* AND *SAMHAIN* AND KNOW AS WE read them that we aren't pronouncing them right. We also know there's something specific meant by them . . . but we don't quite know what that is. And of course we're curious about holidays that have been celebrated for centuries and transmuted into more acceptable contemporary holidays—like Christmas or Candlemas or Halloween. Where did these holidays come from? Was it all orgies and flying on broomsticks?

It's pretty much an accepted fact that people didn't really fly around on broomsticks, and the same goes for the whole orgy thing. Pagan, or Wiccan, holidays are less grotesque and macabre and much more inspirational and joyous than we might imagine.

There are eight traditional pagan holidays, and you'll note that many of them fall on or around a lot of the holidays celebrated by more traditional religions and forms of spirituality. They also occur based on earth events, like the winter solstice or how the earth aligns with certain constellations or other planets in the solar system, and they almost always have something to do with the year's harvest. For that reason, the dates of pagan holidays often aren't fixed, as when the longest night of the season actually falls on December 22 one year, instead of 21. Our calendar isn't that precise, so sometimes we have to be a little flexible. The pagan year runs from October 31 to October

30, and a day begins at sundown the previous evening, so Samhain, the start of the New Year, begins at sundown of October 30.

Each of these holidays, also called sabbats, are celebrated in order to honor a certain time of the year—like harvest or spring—or to honor a particular god or goddess—like Brighid, Lugh, or the Green Man. They are also times of reflection, when a witch might look within and see how she could have done things differently in the past year and how she might continue to evolve, treading lightly and with love through her life.

Your celebration can be as simple or elaborate as you like. It could be as grand and fun as throwing a garden party in honor of Beltane, complete with a maypole, an abundance of flowers, and oat cakes . . . or it could be something just for you, during which you light a rose-scented candle on the summer solstice, reflecting with gratitude on the happiness and prosperity you've enjoyed since winter.

SAMHAIN

Pronounced SOW-in. Also known as All Hallows' Eve or Halloween. Takes place on October 31, the start of the pagan new year.

So many cultures around the world have a day honoring and celebrating the dead. There is the Bon Festival in Japan, Chuseok in Korea, the Festival of Cows in Nepal, the Ghost Festival in China, the Day of the Dead in Mexico, the Turning of the Bones in Madagascar—the list goes on and on. Death is an inescapable part of life, and all of these cultures have come to understand how helpful it is to find a sense of celebration and play in something we may fear and dread, both for ourselves and for others.

On Samhain, the laws of space and time are a little weaker, and the veil that stands between this world and the next is thinner. Not only is it easier to communicate with the dead on Samhain; it is easier to do anything that is normally considered impossible.

Of course, that can be a little dangerous. In our celebrations of the dead, there is always an element of spookiness, of potential threat. It's a good idea to take extra precautions on Samhain. If you go out at night (as most of us will), carry a gris-gris for protection (see page 61), and leave some mandrake or hawthorn around your doors and windows.

COLORS: black, orange, white, and silver

STONES: obsidian, jet, and hematite

HERBS: mugwort, catnip, belladonna, mandrake, and sage

WAYS TO CELEBRATE:
- Leave food offerings on altars and doorsteps, for the dead who may be walking.
- Light a candle in the window to invite the spirits of your loved ones into your home. You can set an extra place at the dinner table for them too, if you like.

- Bury apples alongside the road for wandering spirits that no longer have a home to go to.
- Dress in white or as another gender to confuse spirits that may wish you harm.
- Light a bonfire! Write your name on a stone and throw it in. Check the condition of the stone come morning—depending on how it fared, you will know something of what the coming year will be like for you.

YULE

Pronounced EWE-elle. The day when the darkest half of the year relinquishes its power to the lightest half.
Falls on the winter solstice.

From this day onward, the days grow longer. The Sun King has been reborn. This is a day of uncomplicated celebration—the winter is waning, and it's time to party! Many of the things we now associate with Christmas stem from

Yule, including Christmas trees, the Yule log, and wassailing (i.e., singing Christmas carols).

Of course, these traditions were all slightly different during Yule celebrations—an evergreen tree was never cut down, as it was treasured for its immortality, but boughs of evergreen would be brought inside for the festivities. The Yule log wasn't just a set piece for decoration—it was taken very seriously. You couldn't buy a Yule log; it needed to be given as a gift, from a neighbor or family member, or harvested yourself. The log was traditionally made of ash, and it was *big*. Once it was placed in the fire, the Yule log was decorated with evergreens, holly, and ivy, doused with cider or ale (apples being symbols of the sun), and dusted with flour (representing accomplishment, light, and life) before being set ablaze by a piece of last year's log, which would have been carefully set aside for just this purpose. The log would be kept burning for twelve days—the twelve days of Christmas.

COLORS: red, green, gold, and silver

STONES: ruby, garnet, emerald, and diamond

HERBS: bayberry, evergreen, milk thistle, holly, and mistletoe

WAYS TO CELEBRATE:

- Learn some traditional wassails, like "The Holly and the Ivy," "This Endris Night," or "Gloucestershire Wassail," and sing them to the nearby trees and fields.
- Decorate your home with mistletoe, holly, and ivy.
- Drink a lot of cider. This is traditional.
- Make some form of a Yule log, like setting candles in a log base and lighting them for twelve nights.

IMBOLC

Pronounced IM-bullug. Also called Candlemas or Brighid's Day.
With the help of Hallmark, it has morphed into Valentine's Day.
Takes place on or around February 2.

Imbolc is translated from Gaelic as "in the belly of the mother," since that is where the seeds of rebirth are generated. This time of year is when we look to the end of winter, when lambs are slaughtered, when it is time to bless the seeds and farming tools and prepare to set to work in the coming spring. Brighid (pronounced Breej) is particularly honored on this day, as she is the patron goddess of fire, smithcraft, healing, midwifery, and poetry—all things that will be needed in the coming months.

Imbolc is the time to clean house and be done with hunkering down for the winter. It's time to *get to work.*

COLORS: white, pink, red, and yellow

STONES: amethyst, bloodstone, and garnet

HERBS: angelica, basil, bay laurel, and tansy

WAYS TO CELEBRATE:

- Go for a walk in the woods, hunting for crocuses or other signs of spring.
- Make a Brideo'gas, or a little doll to honor Brighid. They're constructed from straw and decorated with gifts of ribbon or doilies. Fit them with an acorn wand and lay them in the fire overnight. Examine the ashes to see if the wand left a mark—if it did, this will be a good season.
- Make a Brighid's Cross out of straw and rushes for protection.
- Wear a crown of lights, or light candles throughout the house, to welcome the coming warmth into the home.

OSTARA

Pronounced OH-star ah. Celebrates the balance of night and day at the midpoint of spring. Sacred to Eostre, the lunar goddess of fertility. Falls on the spring equinox.

Eostre (pronounced EHS-truh) is not the only deity honored on Ostara, but she is the one that has had the most pronounced influence on our culture. Eggs and rabbits are her symbols . . . so that's where the Easter Bunny comes from. Eostre is also at the root of *estrogen*, which is a nice image to have for an occasionally annoying hormone.

Ostara also honors the Green Man, that mysterious figure permeating so many different cultures around the world, dating back for thousands of years. Every year, he dies and is reborn, symbolizing the rebirth that we experience every year with spring. More than anything, Ostara is about birthing, sprouting, and growth. At this time spring has begun in earnest, and it is apparent in the yellow-green leaves and the delicate blossoms surrounding us.

COLORS: green and yellow

STONES: jasper and emerald

HERBS: early spring flowers in general

WAYS TO CELEBRATE:

- Coloring eggs is technically celebrating Ostara, so carry on.
- Spend the day working in the garden—if you don't have one, volunteer at your neighborhood park.
- Go for a long hike in the woods, assisting new growth wherever you can.
- Make a Green Man by either fashioning a head out of straw or purchasing a foam form from a craft store and covering it with vegetation.

BELTANE

*Pronounced BAY al-TIN-uh. Also known as Roodmas,
Walpurgisnacht, or May Day, it falls on May 1.*

If Ostara is partly about fertility, Beltane is *entirely* about fertility. If pagan holidays did have orgies, they would take place on Beltane. Young couples would spend a night in the woods in true Shakespearean fashion, and couples that had been married for a year and a day could, if they chose, remove their wedding rings along with all the restrictions that those rings impose.

Beltane marks the return of vitality, of passion. It is a celebration of life. It is sensual, but innocent in its sensuality—there is no shame or fear or severity on Beltane. There is nothing but joy.

COLORS: blue, green, and purple

STONES: amethyst, sapphire, and peridot

HERBS: chamomile, wormwood, and lavender

WAYS TO CELEBRATE:

- Rise early in the morning and collect flowers. Weave them into your hair.
- Roll around in the grass with someone you love, and tumble down a hill like a small child.
- Dance around a maypole! It's fun, and harder than it looks!
- Collect wild water, such as dew or fresh water from a stream, and bathe your face in it.
- Build a small bonfire and jump over it, holding hands with the person you love.

LITHA

Pronounced LIE-tha. Also known as Midsummer Night's Eve.
Celebrated on the summer solstice, so on or near June 21.

This is yet another night of celebration, but it is more somber than Beltane. As on Samhain, the veil between this world and the next is quite thin on Litha, and so precautions must be taken. It is a night to celebrate the sun and light, so traditionally bonfires were lit and garlands of herbs tossed onto the flames to honor the Sun God and Queen Mab. This is, of course, an important night for the fairies, as well.

As this night is the shortest of all, it a good one to hold a vigil, watching and waiting for the sun to rise. If you hold steady, you will gain power and control over magic . . . but you risk madness or being whisked away by the fairies.

COLORS: yellow, green, and gold

STONES: emerald and gold

HERBS: mugwort, vervain, chamomile, yarrow, lavender, and thyme

WAYS TO CELEBRATE:

- Light a bonfire and leap over it—the highest leap will determine the height of your crop this year.
- Create a wreath of flowers to toss into the fire.
- Harvest St. John's wort and decorate your home with it, along with rue, trefoil, roses, and vervain.
- Sleep with any of the above under your pillow to encourage good dreams.
- Hold an overnight vigil—or just get up early to watch the sun rise.

LAMMAS

Pronounced luh-MAHS. Also known as Lughnasadh, it is celebrated from August 1 through August 2.

Lammas occurs on the day of the first harvest of the year—so right around the time your local farmer's market starts up in earnest. It is a sign that the hot days of summer are finally coming to an end and the bounty we have worked so hard all year to ensure has finally arrived.

Lammas translates to "loaf-mass;" traditionally, loaves of bread were placed on altars to honor the Green Man, the Sun God (called Lugh in Gaelic), or the Christian God, depending on who was doing the celebrating.

For Lugh, the day has particular significance. Funeral games were held in his honor, though it wasn't his funeral—it was his foster mother, Tailte, who is said to have died of exhaustion after clearing the fields of Ireland for agriculture. The games played on Lammas were contests of strength and skill.

This was also a time for trial marriages; Tailteann marriages were arranged marriages that were given a provisional period of a year and a day—if the marriage was successful after that, great. If not, it was dissolved on the Hills of Separation (actual hills that stand near where the games were traditionally held) as if it had never been.

COLORS: orange, yellow, brown, and green

STONES: carnelian, emerald

HERBS: hops, apples, grains

WAYS TO CELEBRATE:

- Bake a loaf of bread and leave it as an offering for whomsoever you choose.
- Hold a feast, and host some games!
- Make a doll out of a sheaf of corn and hang it in your home until the next harvest, when it should be planted to grow again.
- Perhaps consider taking a significant next step in a relationship, or use Lammas as a day to reflect on how your relationships are working.

MABON

Pronounced MAY-bun. Also known as Alban Elfed or Meán Fómhair,
it is held on the fall equinox, so on or around September 21.

Mabon was a Welsh god of the harvest, a kind of masculine version of Persephone. His holiday celebrates the second harvest, but like Samhain, it is less about joy and accomplishment and more about reflection. On the fall equinox the hours of sunlight are equal to the hours of darkness, so Mabon is about seeking balance—and about respecting the darker aspects of life, since so many of the other holidays are about honoring the sun. It is also a time to give thanks and reflect on all that we have been given throughout the year.

The Scottish refer to the last sheaf of the harvest as "the maiden," and it must be cut down by the youngest female in attendance. Ripe grains were brought in from the field and stored at Mabon, and the casks that beer and wines had been fermenting in since Lammas were opened and consumed. And that, of course, required feasting.

COLORS: red, orange, brown, and gold

STONES: sapphire, lapis lazuli, and yellow agate

HERBS: marigold, milkweed, sage, Solomon's seal, and milk thistle

WAYS TO CELEBRATE:

- Spend your morning in quiet reflection. Acknowledge the darkness within yourself, honoring it and allowing it a seat at your inner table.
- Write a gratitude list.
- Tell stories of death and rebirth—like tales of Odin, Persephone, Mabon, Osiris, Mithras, Dionysus, and of course Jesus Christ.
- Throw a party! Mabon was traditionally a grand feast day, with lots of wine, mead, and beer. Let the darkness have its due, but remember to celebrate the light as well.

WHITE MAGIC

· ·

TO BE HONEST, THERE IS NO SUCH THING AS "WHITE" MAGIC. Magic is magic, and it has no color. As we have seen time and again, it's about *intention*. Love spells, protection spells, truth spells, summoning spells—these could all be considered "white" magic. But if you intend for them to cause harm, then the same spell becomes dark magic.

That brings us to the very obvious next question—what does casting a spell even look like?

Generally speaking, casting a spell looks a lot like it does in the movies. Using herbs or stones and crystals for augmentation, you recite a phrase. You can sit within a pentagram with candles set in the points, if you like—pentagrams have been associated with evil and dark magic, but they aren't really. The pentagram is just a pure mathematical form, and one that Wiccans believe can help focus power. It's all about what feels good and right for you.

Will it work?

You are the only one who can determine that. It certainly won't work if you don't believe it will. There might be other factors that prevent your spell from being effective, too—certain times of day are more powerful than others (sunrise, sunset, the gloaming, midnight), and certain times of the month are as well (new moon, full moon, etc.). If you're tired or unable to focus your energies as powerfully as you might otherwise, your spell will be less effective.

Whatever you do, remember the Rule of Three: whatever you send out into the world will be returned to you threefold.

THE PARTS OF A SPELL

Here are few things you might consider when thinking about casting your spell.

PURIFICATION ◆ Take a cleansing bath, perhaps with some betony, cinquefoil, or hyssop floating in it. Dress however feels right to you—if a long, medieval gown gets you in the right frame of mine, go for it! But remember that a t-shirt and jeans can be just as witchy; it all depends on how you envision yourself, as a witch. Meditate to clear your mind, as well as your body.

CREATING A RITUAL SPACE ◆ A pentagram is one of these, and so is a salt circle. If you don't want to create a physical circle, you can create a psychic one by walking in a circle with a vervain smudge wand or by surrounding a space with clear quartz. If you can perform your spell out of doors, that's great—if not, open a window so that the air can flow freely.

PROTECTION ◆ Drawing and releasing power can invite some negative attention. Protect yourself against spirits or other harmful energies with mandrake, holly, hawthorn, garlic, or betony. You can either drink a tea before you cast the spell or simply have some nearby as part of your ritual space.

INVOCATION ◆ If you choose to, you can invoke the powers of someone or something, like Hecate, the goddess of witchcraft, or simply Spirit or the Universe. You can do this through dance, chanting, or simply with a spoken or silent prayer.

CASTING ◆ You can recite a special phrase (see pages 80–85), or simply state what it is you want to happen. Words only have as much power as you give them, but sometimes speaking a ritualistic phrase helps you feel more powerful, in the same way that dressing appropriately does—and therefore you *are* more powerful.

Utilize whatever you can to enhance the power of your spell. If you're doing a love spell, make your circle or pentagram out of rose quartz and burn myrtle in a smudge stick. Or simply hold tight to a gris-gris as you recite.

Many spells end with the phrase "so mote it be," which translates, essentially, to "so it shall be" or "so must it be." The phrase originated with the Freemasons, but has come to be used frequently within the Wiccan community.

GIVING THANKS ◆ If you asked for assistance from the Divine, be sure to give thanks. You can leave an offering or just bow your head in gratitude—whatever feels right to you.

CLOSING THE CIRCLE ◆ It is important to *finish* your spells, and closing the circle indicates that the spell is complete. If your circle was a psychic one, take your vervain smudge wand and walk in the opposite direction. If you used candles to create a pentagram, blow them out, giving thanks with each one. If you used stones, collect them one by one, again giving thanks.

BASIC SPELLS

The following are suggestions for how to perform a spell, after you've created your ritual space and finished with your invocations. They should be followed by gratitude and closing the circle.

truth spell
✳

If you require a specific truth, write your question on a piece of paper. Use a pimpernel smudge wand, waving it around your face. Let your smudge rest in a bowl, smoldering gently, and use your hands to waft the smoke around you. Light a candle and set your piece of paper, if you used one, on fire, allowing it to turn to ashes in the bowl that holds the smudge wand. Take a tiger's-eye stone and hold it over the smoke. Focus on the stone and recite the following incantation, or another of your choosing:

Let the truth be revealed
Clear away all deceit
Let nothing be concealed
So mote it be

healing spell
✳

Use a garlic or sage smudge wand, and have turquoise, garnet, and clear quartz either on an altar or in your hands. Focus on the person you wish to heal, whether it is yourself or another, and direct your energies particularly toward the injury or illness in question. If you need to be healed, place the stone or stones on the site of injury or illness, or if the person you wish to heal is present, place the stones on their body. Hold your hand over the specific place, and visualize white light and energy flowing from your hand. Recite the following incantation:

> *Let this pain ease*
> *Let my power flow*
> *Let this sickness cease*
> *So mote it be*

protection spell

✴

Make a smudge wand out some combination of mandrake, garlic, cinquefoil, and betony. Use smoky quartz, obsidian, hematite, and pyrite. If you have something specific you want to protect yourself, or another, from, make a doll or symbol of that threat, and surround it with your stones and herbs. If yours is a general protection spell, simply use your smudge wand as you normally would, and hold your stones in your hands. Build a mental wall around yourself or the person you wish to protect. Hold tight to that image, and recite the following incantation:

Let no harm befall
Against all threats, be strong
Let (NAME) be safe behind my wall
So mote it be

abundance spell

✴

Use some combination of vervain, thyme, honeysuckle, and marigold in a smudge wand. Light a candle so that it shines on an image of what you wish to have, whether it is more money, a new car, a new job—whatever it is you're hoping your life will hold. Hold citrine and jade in your hands, or use them as weights on the image. Close your eyes and make that image a reality in your mind. Recite the following incantation:

Let abundance come to me
Allow my dreams to flow
Let me give back more than I receive
So mote it be

summoning spell
✦

Be certain that you have placed extra protection in your circle before you begin. Make a smudge wand of yarrow, mugwort, elecampane, and bella-donna, depending on who or what you want to summon. Hold opal, lapis lazuli, and calcite in your hands. Light a candle so the spirit can find its way. If you are attempting to summon someone specific, have their image present or some token that represents them. Recite the following incantation:

Let my light bring you to me
Follow my voice, come to me
(NAME), I ask you, come to me
So mote it be

banishing spell
✦

If you have summoned something or someone unintentionally, or if you sus-pect that negative energies have become attached to you, make a smudge wand of some combination of wormwood, St. John's wort, hyssop, hellebore, and garlic. Obsidian and hematite can be useful here. Light a candle and recite the following incantation, blowing the candle out when you've finished:

Let this visit be ended
Be gone, and follow me no longer
Let my spirit be mended
So mote it be

self-confidence spell

✦

Begin by writing an affirmation on a small piece of paper. Your affirmation can be whatever you want it to be—whatever you want to celebrate in yourself at that moment or whatever you need a little assistance in celebrating. Make a smudge wand of some combination of thyme, sage, mandrake, lavender, and clover. Light a candle and place aquamarine, azurite, moonstone, citrine, and obsidian in a circle around it. Light your affirmation on fire and place it in the bowl where your smudge wand is smoldering. Recite the following incantation:

Let my true self shine through
I am already all that I need to be
Let me know *that this is true*
So mote it be

love spell

✳

First consider what kind of love spell you want to cast. Is it a general love spell to invite more love into your life? Are you hoping to attract or seal the affections of someone specific? If it is someone specific, write their name on a piece of paper. Make your smudge wand with a combination of myrtle, mistletoe, honeysuckle, dragon's blood, and caraway. If you're hoping to attract someone specific, you might want to add some sage, mandrake, or lemon balm, and if you're casting a spell to improve your marriage, consider using some hawthorn as well. Light a candle and place rose quartz, smoky quartz, jade, and carnelian around it. Scatter rose petals around you, if you like. If you wrote someone's name on your piece of paper, light it on fire and place it in the bowl that holds your smudge wand. Recite the following incantation:

Let me be open to the love that is here
There is much that I do not see
Let (NAME or THE ONE THAT I LOVE) draw me near
So mote it be

PART 3

✦

CASUAL
CLAIRVOYANCE

*Tarot, astrology, palmistry,
and dreams . . . allow the unknown to
guide you, and learn to interpret messages
from within, as well as without.*

TAROT

· ·

HERE'S THE THING ABOUT TAROT—IT CAN BE GENERALLY TRUE OR
it can be creepily on-the-nose. There's no reason why it should work—it's
just a deck of cards with pretty pictures on them—but somehow, every reading has something accurate to say, something that makes you nod your head,
laughing a little as you recognize its truth. And frequently, the feeling you get
after a reading is a sense of relief, an acknowledgment that what you thought
was going on really is going on. Tarot cards tell you what you hope or think or
fear, and then they advise you: What do you want to do? What *should* you do?
How will it all work out?

The first tarot decks surfaced in the mid-1400s and were originally used
for playing card games. It wasn't until the late 1700s that tarot was commonly
used for divination; before that, fortune-tellers used simpler decks with less
precise meanings. Like our current deck of playing cards, tarot cards have
four suits: Cups, Pentacles, Swords, and Wands. Cups represent relationships; Pentacles cover work and money; Swords discuss conflict; and Wands,
of course, are all about magic and creativity. They number ace through ten,
and the "face cards" include the page, knight, queen, and king. These are
known as the Minor Arcana.

A tarot deck has twenty-two additional cards, which are known as the
Major Arcana. They move in a cycle, beginning with the Fool, passing through
Death and the Tower (which don't mean quite what you think they do), and
ending with the World—a card of fulfillment.

The wonderful thing about tarot is that anyone can do a reading, because it's all about intention. The cards can tell you nothing you don't already know, because you are giving your energy to the cards and they are merely reflecting it back to you. If you ask the cards a question, they will simply confirm what you already know to be true—whether you wanted to admit it to yourself or not. Remember, they're just pieces of paper with pictures on them. Any power they have comes from what you bring to them.

Learning tarot can feel like a lot of memorization—each deck comes with a book explaining the meaning of each card, and that's very helpful. But as you practice, and as you get to know your deck and how it speaks to you, you'll find that each card has a slightly different, specific meaning that can only be interpreted by you. Say, for instance, that your tarot reader is a mother, and she associates the Fool card with her child. If she pulls that card, she won't interpret it to mean that you are an idiot. Since this is her deck, and since she is the one doing the reading, then in this case the Fool card means innocence and possibility.

In order for the reading to be as powerful as it can be, you need to have a deck that provokes specific associations within you. But when it comes to choosing a deck, there are so many options it can seem overwhelming. The traditional Rider-Waite and Aleister Crowley Thoth are the most common, but that doesn't mean that they will be the best for you. Look for a deck that attracts you, that is evocative, that makes you *want* to do a reading. A deck that you like is one that will respond to you, one that will speak to you.

Interpreting tarot requires balancing knowledge and intuition; the archetypes in each card provide history and grounding to your reading, but as a reader you can go deeper than that. Listen to your instincts and you'll find that you can learn and see so much more.

THE SUITS

cups

✳

The suit of Cups is about relationships and how our emotions play into our connection—or lack thereof—with those around us. When you see a spread that is dominated by Cups, there is obviously something going on with one of your primary relationships, but it's also an indication that you're being driven by your emotions, rather than by logic or thought.

This is by no means a bad thing, necessarily—remember, there are no "bad" cards—but it can have a downside. If you are driven only by your emotions, reason gets left behind, leading to unrealistic expectations and self-absorbed behavior.

The Cups' element is water, and how you interpret that will inform your understanding of the cards. Is the cup the self, and water what our relationships with others bring us? Or do you understand the symbolism differently?

pentacles

*

The suit of Pentacles—also known as Coins or Disks—is the suit of work and prosperity. How you define that work depends on the person the reading is for—this could be a job, or it could be the work we do around the home, maintaining our family and relationships. It depends on the context, but, generally speaking, Pentacles refer to work for monetary gain.

Because they are externally focused, they may also reflect our relationship with the world outside our own inner circle—so outside the group that the Cups would speak to.

The element of Pentacles is earth, and as such, it's a very *practical* suit, which seems odd in tarot—but at the same time, it's refreshing to see our most basic needs and goals discussed and held with the same respect as our creativity and relationships. The downside of being Pentacles-focused is obvious—greed and losing sight of what's really important.

swords

*

A spread made up almost entirely of Swords will appear in everyone's life at some point. We all experience conflict. We all have battles to fight.

The Swords aren't literal here—instead, what cuts is the sharpness of logic and intellect. Sometimes our minds are at war with our hearts, and

sometimes, our hearts are in danger from the force of another's cold, hard logic, or vice versa.

The element of Swords is air, perhaps because the battles fought by Swords are seen from above, where the air is cold and thin and everything seems black and white. But again, there are no "bad" cards, and this is not a "bad" suit. Seeing things clearly is not a bad thing, and while logic and justice may hurt, they are necessary. Swords will keep you on the straight and narrow, so to speak. And that is usually a good thing.

wands

✳

The element of Wands is fire, which may seem counter-intuitive for a suit about creativity until you take a closer look. Fire, in the form of lava, is *literal* creation—land is created when lava hits the ocean. But creativity can also be a destructive force—like a forest fire, if it is not controlled, it can be damaging. Consider J. Robert Oppenheimer quoting the Bhagavad Gita, "Now I am become death, the destroyer of worlds."

Usually, though, we think of Wands as the spark, the magical moment of beginning, rather than the conflagration. They are about *your* creativity and how you bring your true self out into the open. If you encounter a spread dominated by Wands, then that means it's time to pursue that creative dream. That may not necessarily mean taking a painting class or writing a novel—though it might! It might also mean starting your own business, taking a risk, even having a child. What's important is putting your authentic self out into the world.

THE MAJOR ARCANA

⓪ THE FOOL: *Childlike Idealism, Innocence, Blind Stupidity.* The Fool is just setting out on his journey, and he has unlimited potential. If the Fool appears in your reading, consider starting something new. Be spontaneous, and embrace the "foolishness" in yourself.

① THE MAGICIAN: *Mastery, Magic, Power.* The Magician can do anything—and he will. This is a card of action and a card of ability. You can achieve what you want.

② THE HIGH PRIESTESS: *Unconscious, Dreaming, Mystical.* The High Priestess stands opposed to/complements the Magician. Where he steps forward with reason, she steps back to allow her intuition to speak. Listen to the space between.

③ THE EMPRESS: *Earth Mother, Creation, Fertility.* The Empress is very sensual and very caring. She tells you to nourish others and to nourish yourself, particularly through nature.

④ THE EMPEROR: *Tradition, Authority, Rules.* The Emperor is a father figure in a very rigid, traditional sense; this is the father that is the breadwinner and the one who delivers punishment when it is warranted. When the Emperor appears, rules and regulations are paramount, because they provide us with the structure we need.

⑤ THE HIEROPHANT: *Belief, Learning, Conformity.* The Hierophant believes in education, but only in established, widely accepted facts. The Hierophant frequently represents the Church, but it can also mean whatever group you are most often expected to conform to.

⑥ **THE LOVERS:** *Duality, Love, Harmony.* The Lovers are often literal and romantic, but they can also refer to a difficult decision, one in which the right choice isn't always clear—because you want both, together.

⑦ **THE CHARIOT:** *Balance, Self-Control, War Within.* There are two horses (or sphinxes, or something else, depending on your deck) pulling the Chariot, and you must master both of them. If you do, you will win.

⑧ **STRENGTH:** *Resilience, Fortitude, Self-Confidence.* If the Chariot requires a heavy hand, true Strength requires a light touch. Being someone you and others can depend on requires patience and compassion, as well as confidence in yourself.

⑨ **THE HERMIT:** *Spirituality, Solitude, Wisdom.* The Hermit retreats into himself, looking for an understanding of *something more.* If he appears, it's time to be introspective. Give yourself some alone time and search within yourself for answers.

⑩ **WHEEL OF FORTUNE:** *Change, Destiny, Cycles.* As the seasons change, so does the Wheel of Fortune. Change is the only constant in our lives, and the Wheel speaks to how, with every cycle, we are moving in a specific—even fated—direction.

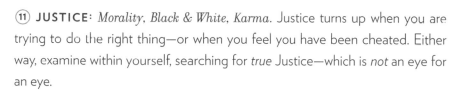

⑪ **JUSTICE:** *Morality, Black & White, Karma.* Justice turns up when you are trying to do the right thing—or when you feel you have been cheated. Either way, examine within yourself, searching for *true* Justice—which is *not* an eye for an eye.

⑫ **THE HANGED MAN:** *Sacrifice, Self-Awareness, Knowledge.* The Hanged Man is another union of opposites, and it demands something that seems impossible—that we gain control through surrender. It is in the act of letting go of what we want that we allow it to come to us.

⑬ **DEATH**: *Change, Transformation, Endings.* Even though it doesn't mean literal death, the Death card is always frightening—because change is frightening. Something is coming to an end, and something new is beginning. A door is closing—but a window is opening.

⑭ **TEMPERANCE**: *Moderation, Compromise, Self-Control.* So many cards in the tarot are about duality, and Temperance's take on duality is the most comforting, if a little boring. She brings opposing forces together and teaches them to respect one another (including forces within yourself). It isn't easy—this kind of balance requires hard work and self-restraint.

⑮ **THE DEVIL**: *Self-Deception, The Monster Within, Ignorance.* If there *were* a "bad" card in tarot, this would be it. But this isn't about literal evil in your life, it is about a bad situation—usually one of your own creation. The Devil insists that you look closely at your life and see where you have gone wrong.

⑯ **THE TOWER**: *Destruction, Betrayal, Starting Over.* If Death is about change, at least it's a change that we can see coming. The Tower burns suddenly, destroying everything you thought you held dear. It could simply mean a new perspective—or it could mean a drastic alteration in life circumstances. Either way, the Tower will slap you upside the head.

⑰ **THE STAR**: *Hope, Inspiration, New Possibilities.* After the Tower, the Star is a balm. As bad as things can get, there is always a way out—there is always hope. When the Star appears, take a breath and allow the peacefulness and vastness of the universe to calm and inspire you.

⑱ **THE MOON:** *Illusion, Mystery, Possibility—Positive or Negative.* The world looks different by moonlight—and different can be scary and disorienting. But it doesn't have to be. When the Moon is out, anything is possible. Let yourself be open to fantasy. Allow the impossible.

⑲ **THE SUN:** *Clarity, Confidence, Surety.* And now we've returned to the light. There is no ambiguity under the Sun—and you should bask in that certainty. The Sun tells you that you are brilliant, energetic, and successful.

⑳ **JUDGMENT:** *Looking Back, Conviction, Redemption.* You could interpret Judgment in a harsh light—determining right or wrong—or you could instead use *good judgment* and meditate on the choices you have made without condemning yourself or others. Sometimes really looking at something you have done can absolve you of any guilt you feel.

㉑ **THE WORLD:** *Completion, Fulfillment, Unity.* The World completes the cycle of the tarot. You have finished what you set out to do, and you should savor the unity that you have found within yourself—you have brought together those opposing dualities in a way that is lasting, that has made you whole.

THREE-CARD SPREAD

This is the simplest spread (unless you're doing a very basic one-card reading), but it offers so much within such a contained form. Have the person you're reading for shuffle the cards until they feel satisfied, and then hold the deck close to their heart and ask any question they may have. If they don't have a question, that's fine, and if you're doing a reading for yourself, you should of course shuffle for yourself.

Fan the cards out in a line so that each card is visible. If a certain card seems to want to stay hidden, let it. Have the person you're reading for choose three cards, or if you're reading for yourself, let your intuition help you to choose. If the answer to your question seems hidden from you, perhaps choose a hidden card. Sometimes your card will make your fingers tingle, or it might feel slightly warm beneath your hands.

Lay the three cards faceup. You can interpret them, from left to right, as past, present, and future, as is commonly done. But if you're doing a reading for yourself, you of course already know your past and much of your present. So consider asking the cards, "What is going on for me, consciously?" "What is going on for me, unconsciously?" and "What should I focus on today?"

GUIDANCE SPREAD

This spread goes deeper and is useful when you're facing a particular challenge or having trouble seeing all sides of an issue. A guidance spread will help you examine a situation from a broader perspective.

As before, shuffle and hold the cards close to your heart as you ask your question. You'll draw eight cards, the first alone, and the following seven in a row above it.

FIRST CARD ◆ This card represents your primary concern, the issue at hand.

SECOND CARD ◆ What's your motivation? Why are you looking for guidance here?

THIRD CARD ◆ This card represents the area(s) in your life that you feel anxious about.

FOURTH CARD ◆ This card points out elements in your situation that you may not be aware of.

FIFTH CARD ◆ This card will give you the information you require in order to overcome your apprehensions.

SIXTH CARD ◆ This card will help you feel comfortable letting your anxieties go.

SEVENTH CARD ◆ This card will advise you in how to move forward.

EIGHTH CARD ◆ This card tells you how it could all work out in the end, if you follow the path.

ASTROLOGY

$\cdots\cdots\cdots\cdots\cdots\cdots\cdots\cdots\cdots\cdots\cdots\cdots\cdots$

ARIES, TAURUS, GEMINI, CANCER, LEO, VIRGO, LIBRA, SCORPIO, Sagittarius, Capricorn, Aquarius, Pisces—we all know our signs, and we know that we can read different bits of information or advice on a monthly, weekly, or even daily basis relating to them. We've all heard the phrase "Mercury in retrograde," and we know it's probably a bad thing. Beyond that, we leave it to the professionals, because it all seems pretty overwhelming.

The truth is, it *is* overwhelming. There's a reason why, for centuries, astrologers were so valued by rulers for the advice and information they could give. There is a lot to keep track of, but it's not that complicated if you break it down. Astrology is simply using the movements of celestial bodies (like the planets and certain constellations) to make determinations about what is going on here on earth. It's a practice that has been around for millennia and, up until the Enlightenment, was taken quite seriously all over the world, though practices differed from culture to culture.

Western astrology is centered around the date of birth and based on Ptolemy's *Tetrabiblos*, which is considered the most authoritative text on astrology and itself based on Babylonian astrology. One thing to bear in mind is that cycles and changes in the heavens are merely *reflective* of cycles and changes on earth and in one's life—they are not causative. They happen simultaneously, because that is how the universe works, but one doesn't directly impact the other. We simply use the movements of the stars to interpret and understand what's happening to us here on earth.

The zodiac refers to a belt of twelve constellations that the sun and the planets move through in the course of a year. Those twelve constellations each have a certain personality, which translates to the characteristics of your zodiac sign. Each sign is ruled by a particular celestial body—the sun, the moon, or one of the planets—though every celestial body travels through each sign at some point during the year. The signs are organized according to the seasons, rather than the calendar year, with spring coming first—so, in order, they are Aries, Taurus, Gemini, Cancer, Leo, Virgo, Libra, Scorpio, Sagittarius, Capricorn, Aquarius, and Pisces.

The signs fall into the elemental categories of fire, water, earth, and air. Although each sign has its own personality traits, it will also have many traits in common with other signs of its element. Each sign will also be generally compatible with its fellow elemental signs.

Just to be confusing, there are also twelve Houses, which have nothing to do with the twelve signs. A House simply refers to an area of your life—like your family, your work, your identity, and so forth—and is determined by the earth's rotation around its axis. The positions of each of the signs and the celestial bodies rotate through the Houses, so that at any given time, each House will be ruled by a different sign and celestial body.

So what do we do with all of this? What does an astrological chart do, anyway?

Most astrological charts reflect how the stars were aligned on the day you were born. A natal chart will give an indication of what your life will be like, a better understanding of who you are. But as it is only one day, albeit a very important day, it cannot give you the whole picture. Instead, doing a chart on a monthly, weekly, or even daily basis can provide a more specific and clear understanding of what is going on in your life right now and how to act accordingly.

THE ELEMENTS AND THEIR SIGNS

fire

✦

Fire signs are invariably powerful, energetic, and full of life. They are highly creative and charismatic, drawing others to them. They are inspiring, passionate, and feel things deeply.

ARIES. Someone born under Aries is a quick thinker and a born leader. Active and brave, they are competitive, efficient, and energetic. However, they can be impulsive, impatient, or aggressive at times.

March 21–April 19 ✦ RULER: Mars ✦ BEST PAIRED WITH: Libra

LEO. A Leo is creative and individualistic. Passionate and generous, they love life and adore solving problems. They can be seen as arrogant or a performer, as a Leo requires applause. Leos want to be seen for who they really are.

July 23–August 22 ✦ RULER: Sun ✦ BEST PAIRED WITH: Aquarius

SAGITTARIUS. A Sagittarius wants to change the world. They are philosophical and deep thinkers, but they can easily transform thought into action. They are intensely curious and love to travel, but can be impatient and tactless.

November 22–December 21 ✦ RULER: Jupiter ✦ BEST PAIRED WITH: Gemini

earth

✦

Earth signs get things done. They are dedicated and responsible—the epitome of "down-to-earth." They are loyal, patient, and hardworking, though also naturally conservative; they don't like to take risks. They are, however, quite ambitious and tend to get what they want.

TAURUS: A Taurus works hard and loves to bask in the fruit of that labor—and deservedly so. They are sensual and tactile, and often surrounded by beautiful material possessions. They are stubborn, but in the best way, and will stick with a project—or a person—until the very end. They can be overprotective and uncompromising at times.

April 20–May 20 ✦ RULER: Venus ✦ BEST PAIRED WITH: Scorpio

VIRGO. Empathetic and insightful, a Virgo treads carefully. They lead an organized life and leave nothing to chance. Virgos are polite and health-conscious, at one with nature. They can be shy and overly critical, both of themselves and of others.

August 23–September 22 ✦ RULER: Mercury ✦ BEST PAIRED WITH: Pisces

CAPRICORN: Often considered the most serious sign in the zodiac, Capricorns are independent and professional, but their families are of paramount importance. They are very responsible and practical, with excellent self-control. They can be a little condescending and unforgiving at times.

December 22–January 19 ✦ RULER: Saturn ✦ BEST PAIRED WITH: Cancer

air

✦

Air signs are kind of like the best aspects of the Internet. They are extremely intelligent and excellent at communication, but they are so restless that they are constantly moving on to the next idea, and the next, as they hunger for more information. They are social and chatty, but they value truth and realism above all. That combination allows them to see both sides of an issue in a balanced way.

GEMINI: A Gemini can be a little confusing, in that sometimes they are fun and playful and social, but other times, they can be restless, introspective, and indecisive. They are excellent communicators, and excel at art, writing, and journalism. They are fascinated by the world and want to share that joy.

May 21–June 20 ✦ RULER: Mercury ✦ BEST PAIRED WITH: Sagittarius

LIBRA: A Libra is crucial to a successful society—they are peaceful and fair, and value partnership and cooperation. They have a keen mind and are easily inspired by the goodness and beauty in the world. A Libra might occasionally have a hard time being alone and may be so anxious to keep the peace that they will allow a grudge to develop before confronting the problem.

September 23–October 22 ✦ RULER: Venus ✦ BEST PAIRED WITH: Aries

AQUARIUS: Occasionally an Aquarius will come off as reserved, but they are simply very deep thinkers. They are excellent problem-solvers and love to help others, but they do require alone time to recharge. They value their freedom and need to get to know someone before they are allowed too close. They can be a little temperamental or aloof at times.

January 20—February 18 ✦ RULER: Uranus ✦ BEST PAIRED WITH: Leo

water

Water signs can be kind of unpredictable, but one thing is certain—they always feel things deeply, even if it doesn't always show. They are sensitive, intuitive, and empathetic, as well as imaginative and independent.

CANCER: Like all water signs, Cancers care deeply—and in this case, they care most about their families. They are extremely loyal and experience another's suffering as their own. They can have trouble controlling their emotions and can sometimes be moody or insecure.

June 21–July 22 ✦ RULER: Moon ✦ BEST PAIRED WITH: Capricorn

SCORPIO: A Scorpio is determined and decisive. Because of this, they are excellent leaders and, unlike some water signs, have no trouble feeling and expressing their emotions. They are great at keeping secrets (and a little mysterious themselves) and have an excellent business sense. They can be a little suspicious and jealous sometimes.

October 23–November 21 ✦ RULER: Pluto ✦ BEST PAIRED WITH: Taurus

PISCES: Pisces are very friendly and genuinely compassionate and caring—their selflessness makes them wonderful friends. They are wise, gentle, and very tolerant of other people's differences. They are very musical and have lasting and deep relationships.

February 19–March 20 ✦ RULER: Neptune ✦ BEST PAIRED WITH: Virgo

THE CELESTIAL BODIES

SUN: As the center of our solar system, the Sun is essentially the center of *our* universe. It provides us with light, life, and represents our ego, our health, and our pride. The Sun is an authority, usually the authority we have over ourselves and others. The Sun makes its journey through the zodiac once per year, spending about a month with each sign.

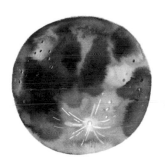

MOON: The Moon also provides light, but it is a mysterious light, and so the Moon represents our intuition, our deepest feelings, and our private lives. The Moon is connected to our familial history, our roots—and our ability to connect with our emotions. The Moon takes only twenty-eight days to travel through the zodiac, spending two to three days with each sign.

MERCURY: Mercury is an excellent communicator, but mainly in the realm of rational thought. Mercury revolves around research, learning, decision-making, and the sharing of information. When Mercury goes retrograde (meaning when it appears to be moving backward across the night sky—though mind you, that's just an optical illusion caused by the differences in the speed of its orbit with respect to Earth's), it scrambles its ability to disseminate that information, causing all kinds of confusion. If Mercury is in retrograde, definitely hold off signing any important contracts or making any big decisions. It also wreaks particular havoc with the technology of communication, so expect your iPhone to crap out on you. Since Mercury is so close to the Sun, its journey across the zodiac is very similar in length and time.

VENUS: As you might expect, Venus represents love, beauty, and pleasure. Venus is alluring and receptive, but not aggressive. Venus can be a little manipulative, but only in a short-term, hedonistic way; thinking about consequences and making careful plans are not Venus' way. But when Venus retrogrades, then that's a time to reassess and think about whom or what we truly value. Venus generally takes about ten to twelve months to travel across the zodiac, spending a few weeks with each sign.

MARS: Mars is a force of nature. Its energy is aggressive, energetic, competitive, and brave. Mars governs war, of course, but war in all forms, including sports, arguments, and any kind of conflict. When Mars goes retrograde, though, it's time to retreat and regroup. Mars takes approximately two years to circle the zodiac, spending six or seven weeks with each sign.

JUPITER: Jupiter is a planet of vision, faith, optimism, and wisdom. As our largest gas giant, it casts a powerful shadow of good fortune—because of this, Jupiter is sometimes known as the Great Benefactor. Jupiter encourages us to seek out the new—externally, through travel, but also inwardly, as we learn something we hadn't considered before and feel confident to explore. When Jupiter is in retrograde, that forward expansion turns inward; you may find yourself planning and replanning without actually getting started. Jupiter takes twelve years to travel the zodiac, and it sits with each sign for a full year.

SATURN: Called the Great Teacher, Saturn is a planet of ambition and productivity, but also of caution and responsibility. Saturn is not a dreamer; instead it forces us to confront reality, bringing maturity and the values of patience, consideration, structure, and sacrifice. When this planet is in retrograde, we have the

opportunity to go back and revisit things we might have wanted to do differently, to consider other ways of doing things. Saturn takes twenty-nine years to go across the zodiac and stays in each sign for two and a half years.

URANUS: If Saturn teaches us to be responsible and think things through, Uranus helps us learn to love the unexpected. It rules the future and all new technology. Anything innovative, idiosyncratic, or experimental falls under Uranus' umbrella. And Uranus encourages us to think as far outside the box as possible—maybe even breaking the box. When Uranus is in retrograde, you may experience a shift inside yourself, where a change that you had been resisting suddenly becomes more appealing—even necessary. Uranus takes eighty-four years to circle the zodiac and stays with a sign for seven of those years—making those seven years very creative, indeed.

NEPTUNE: Lovely Neptune is the planet of inspiration. Like the Moon, it governs intuition, dreams, the subconscious, and the magical. But Neptune goes deeper than the Moon does, making us purer, more refined. It urges us to be more than we are, to not accept Saturn's reality, but instead strive for greatness. When Neptune is in retrograde, how- 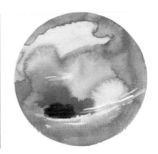 ever, reality comes knocking, and you might receive a wake-up call. It's a great time to make decisions about what is really important to you. Neptune circles the zodiac over the course of 146 years, staying with each sign for fourteen years.

PLUTO: Not yet demoted from full planetary status in astrology, Pluto rules transformation, rebirth, and metamorphosis. Pluto reigns over all that is unseen or buried, including secrets, the unconscious workings of society, and planning. Pluto can be a bit unpredictable, sometimes helping you to hide, and other times revealing all. When it is in retrograde, Pluto asks you to look inward, particularly at the parts of yourself you may not like so much. Is it time to transform? Pluto takes 246 years to travel around the zodiac. Its eccentric orbit makes its stay with each sign uneven—sometimes it visits for eleven years, sometimes for thirty-two.

THE TWELVE HOUSES

FIRST HOUSE ◆ *The House of the Self.* It includes your personality, your physical body, your appearance, and your self-image. The First House reveals your ascendant sign, the sign rising on the horizon. For natal charts, this sign can be equally as important as your birth sign in understanding yourself.

SECOND HOUSE ◆ *The House of Worth.* It refers to money, possessions, what you value, and your self-esteem. The sign that rests in your Second House reflects how you spend your money and your attitude toward your finances and your possessions.

THIRD HOUSE ◆ *The House of Intellect.* It drives your communication skills and your understanding of the world. It also governs your relationship with your immediate surroundings, including your neighborhood, your siblings, and short journeys.

FOURTH HOUSE ◆ *The House of the Home.* It includes your literal house—where it is, what it looks like—along with what makes your home, be that your spouse and children, a roommate, or whomever else you might share your space with. It also determines your relationship with your parents.

FIFTH HOUSE ◆ *The House of Love.* It includes both romantic love and the love you may feel for your children. It also rules creativity, self-expression, and pleasure.

SIXTH HOUSE ◆ *The House of Work.* It includes your job, but also the work that you do in every aspect of your daily life—shopping, cleaning, cooking, etc. Diet, fitness, and exercise fall under this category, as well—the work we do to maintain our bodies.

SEVENTH HOUSE ◆ *The House of Partnership.* It often refers to marriage, but may also encompass work relationships—it is involved whenever two parties agree to work together toward a common goal. There will often be conflicts in those kinds of situations, so your enemies as well as your allies fall under this house.

EIGHTH HOUSE ◆ *The House of Transformation.* This house can be a little confusing—it relates to money, but in the way that we exchange money with others. Investments, mortgages, gifts, taxes, child support—all of these fall under the Eighth House. Physical sex and reproduction occur here, as well. The theme is change; under the Eighth House, we interact with others and change because of that interaction.

NINTH HOUSE ◆ *The House of Understanding.* If the Third House is about intellect, the Ninth House goes deeper, to a more philosophical and spiritual place. The Ninth House governs dreams, visions, ideas, ethics, and rituals. Long-distance travel, distant relatives, and higher education are all in its purview.

TENTH HOUSE ◆ *The House of Status.* The areas in which we excel professionally and within the community reside in this house. The Tenth House helps us understand how our colleagues and neighbors see us.

ELEVENTH HOUSE ◆ *The House of Friendship.* This house is more specifically about community, about the way we relate to those we come together with in a group.

TWELFTH HOUSE ◆ *The House of the Subconscious.* If the First House is about our own self-image, the Twelfth House is the self that we cannot always see or recognize. It rules our dreams and our intuition, as well as our secrets and our sorrows.

HOW TO CREATE A NATAL CHART

For a real, in-depth natal chart—one that calculates angles of ascension and how the signs and planets interact with each other—go to the professionals (and there are lots of websites that will do your chart for free). But you can dive in yourself for just a taste and to take a look at how the signs influence the houses.

① Draw three concentric circles on a piece of paper. Using a ruler, divide the circle into twelve equal parts, like slicing a pizza into twelve pieces.

② Determine your ascendant sign. This sign is whatever was rising over the horizon on the date and at the exact time of your birth. Find it by looking it up in an ephemeris (a chart that tracks the positions of celestial bodies at any given time) or by looking it up online. Position this information at eight o'clock on your chart. This is your First House (The House of Self).

③ Follow the natural order of the signs (see page 102) as you fill in each of the remaining eleven spaces. So if you had Aries in your First House, you would put Taurus in the Second House, Gemini in the Third House, and so forth.

What does all this tell you? If you're a Libra, but your ascendant sign is Gemini, then that might explain why the characteristics of Libras have never seemed to accurately describe you, because you're really a combination of both. If you've got Pisces in your Second House (The House of Worth), then you might have a better understanding of why you're always loaning people money. If your Fifth House of love is ruled by Taurus, you'll know why you are always so stubborn, getting into fights with those you adore the most.

Or it might tell you nothing you don't already know, and so it may just be a fun exercise—something to do on a rainy day.

Turn to page 150 to fill in your own natal chart.

PALMISTRY

· ·

IT IS INTERESTING THAT SO MANY PROPHESYING PRACTICES date back centuries and centuries. Is this because we felt so lost and confused then, that we more desperately needed to know the answers? Or is it because we were less skeptical and more readily sought answers because we believed they were available?

In any case, palmistry is no exception. The art of reading palms dates back to Babylonia, ancient Greece, China, and India, among other places, until it was heavily suppressed by the Catholic Church in the Middle Ages. The Church ranked it as one of the seven "forbidden arts," putting it right up there with necromancy and fire magic. Compared to those two, simple palm-reading seems fairly harmless.

But the Church's efforts to suppress palmistry were very successful until the mid-1800s, when people started taking the practice seriously again. It became regulated by the Chirological Society of Great Britain, so that certain lines on a palm would always be interpreted the same way, no matter who was doing the reading. But, like tarot and astrology, palmistry tells more about the personality of the bearer of the palm, and less about their future, though there is a little of that sprinkled in.

There is reason to believe that there is *something* behind palmistry. The practice of fingerprinting, for instance, reminds us that no two hands are exactly alike. And while the eyes may be the windows to the soul, the hands are a lot easier to read. We do *everything* with our hands, and they bear the evidence of that. The callus from where you hold your pen, the way you bite

115

your nails, the swelling around a wedding ring, or the tan line from where one used to be. . . . the scars, the burns, everything—the evidence of our lives is in our hands. We have them to thank for our place outside of the food chain. It's no wonder that palmistry has hung on for so long, despite the efforts to suppress it.

There are two branches of palmistry: Chiromancy, which deals with the lines on the palm, is what usually comes to mind when we think about palm-reading. But there is also chirognomy, which looks at the shape and texture of the hands, including the fingers and thumb.

Each hand will tell a reader something different. The nondominant hand represents the person's inherited traits—what they were born with and how they came into the world. The dominant hand shows how life has changed that person. Watch for the differences between the two hands.

CHIROMANCY

There are three major lines—the life line, the heart line, and the head line—and several minor lines, as well as a number of mounts and markings to read with chiromancy. If you read the various descriptions here and then look at your palm, you'll find that several of them may apply; for example, your life line might be short, forked, and shallow. The art of palmistry is not just in being able to see the lines clearly, but also in how you interpret the information you are given, so that you can tell someone with a short, forked, and shallow life line that they are better at overcoming challenges than they think they are, and that they will need to harness that ability soon, as their life is about to change.

Remember, too, that the lines will be different on each hand and you should take both hands into account, though the nondominant hand will generally reveal more.

the major lines

THE LIFE LINE ◆ This line tells you a great deal about your life—but it doesn't tell you when you are going to die or anything like that. Instead, the life line describes the kind of life you will have and are having—your relationships, your health, your very existence.

> LONG: A long life line indicates a healthy and well-balanced person.
> SHORT: This line communicates that the person is good at overcoming challenges. Note: It does *not* mean a short life.
> FAINT: Low energy, perhaps unwilling to take chances.
> DEEP: A smooth and easy life.

BROKEN: A life line with a break in it signifies that there has been a major disruption, like an illness or an accident. If the break occurs in both hands, it means that the disruption was more severe. The closer to the wrist the break is, the younger the person was when the disruption occurred.

FORKED: A fork marks a change in lifestyle.

CHAINED: Crisscrossing lines point to a troubled path.

MULTIPLES: If the person has more than one life line moving along essentially the same path, that can mean they have a true soul partner in life, like a twin, friend, or life partner.

THE HEART LINE ◆ Also known as the love line, or the mensal line, this gives hints to the person's emotional state, as well as their relationships with others.

LONG: This would suggest the person is balanced and open, but perhaps a little starry-eyed.

OVEREXTENDED: If the line reaches all the way across the palm, it indicates that the person might have codependent tendencies.

SHORT: Self-centered.

DEEP: Stressed by relationships.

FAINT: Doesn't place much importance on emotions or relationships.

STRAIGHT: Somewhat passive in relationships.

CURVED: Emotional, intuitive.

WAVY: May have trouble with commitment.

BROKEN: The person may have experienced or will experience an emotional trauma.

FORKED. Practical, good at maintaining balance.

CHAINED. Easily hurt, may suffer from depression.

BRANCHES GOING UP. This person has strong relationships.

BRANCHES GOING DOWN. This person suffers from heartbreak on occasion.

THE HEAD LINE ◆ The line of wisdom goes deeper than just learning—it also reveals information about the person's psychological makeup, as well as their intuitive abilities.

STARTS FROM SAME POINT AS THE LIFE LINE: Such a shape indicates a strong will.

LONG: A long line suggests intelligence, a good memory, and a willingness to think things through.

OVEREXTENDED: If the line extends across the entire palm, the person is likely highly successful and brave—though possibly also somewhat selfish.

SHORT: Practical, no-nonsense.

STRAIGHT: Realistic, good attention to detail. Not much imagination.

CURVED: Idealistic, intuitive, and imaginative.

WAVY: Points to inner conflict between the person's thoughts and actions. May be untrustworthy.

DEEP: Sensible, with an excellent memory.

FAINT. Daydreams, has trouble concentrating.

BROKEN: Signifies inconsistency and perhaps mental exhaustion.

FORKED: Called a "writer's fork" or a "lawyer's fork." This person enjoys debate, has an excellent imagination, and communicates clearly.

BRANCHES GOING UP: Professional success.

BRANCHES GOING DOWN: Struggle, disappointment, or depression at some point in the person's life.

the minor lines

Not all of these lines will be present on every hand, but if they are there, they indicate something more specific about the person. These are not all the Minor Lines, but this list covers the most common ones. See page 114 for further reference.

SUN LINE ◆ Also known as the Apollo line, indicates that the person is creative, successful, and self-confident.

BRACELET LINES ◆ Also known as rascette lines, they indicate longevity. The more of these lines someone has, and the clearer those lines are, the longer and healthier that person's life will be.

FATE LINE ◆ Also known as the Line of Destiny, it indicates the person's life path. This line refers to events that the person has no control over, obstacles that must be faced.

GIRDLE OF VENUS ◆ This line indicates a very emotional person, one who experiences both extreme highs and extreme lows.

LINE OF HEALTH ◆ This line may say something about the person's health, but its presence more likely speaks to skills as a healer, either emotionally or physically.

INTUITION LINE ◆ This person is highly sensitive and may even possess psychic abilities, but has difficulty in crowds.

mounts

✦

Mounts are the bumps of flesh on the palms. They may be more or less pronounced on your hand. See page 114 for reference.

MOUNT OF VENUS ✦ This bump relates to love and passions. If it's present but not unusually pronounced, the person is healthy, has positive relationships, and appreciates the beauty in the world. If it's elevated, the person is self-indulgent. If it's flat, the person does not have a strong connection to their family.

MOUNT OF JUPITER ✦ This mount relates to the ego, to how we want to be perceived, and to success. If it is present but not unusually pronounced, the person is compassionate, generous, and has a positive outlook. If it is elevated, the person is self-centered and likes to be in control of others. If it is flat, the person is lacking in self-confidence.

MOUNT OF SATURN ✦ This shape refers to patience, duty, and responsibility. If it is present but not unusually pronounced, the person is friendly, independent, and takes their responsibilities seriously. If it is elevated, the person may be depressed or isolated from others. If it is flat, the person might be disorganized and not very self-aware.

MOUNT OF APOLLO ✦ Also known of the Mount of the Sun, this bump relates to self-assurance. If it is present but not unusually pronounced, the person is outgoing and flexible. If it is elevated, the person might have a jealous nature. If it is flat, the person might be shy and indecisive.

MOUNT OF MERCURY ◆ This elevation points to success, and also to the ability to read people. If it is present but not unusually pronounced, the person is successful in business and an excellent communicator. If it is elevated, the person may be a bit greedy. If it is flat, the person might have trouble reading social cues and may be unambitious.

MOUNT OF LUNA ◆ Also known as the Mount of the Moon, it relates to intuition, imagination, and creativity. If it is present but not unusually pronounced, the person is artistic and thrives when immersed in nature, particularly by the sea. If it is elevated, the person might dwell overlong on fantasies. If it is flat, the person might be imaginative, but prefers to be private.

markings

✦

Of course we all have other marks all over our hands, sometimes on the lines themselves. These add a deeper layer of meaning to the lines, as a way of interpreting them more specifically. Stand-alone markings have meaning as well.

BREAKS ✦ Most lines have breaks in them. They don't necessarily signify anything negative; they simply mark a life lived, an interruption in the flow of energy, which happens to all of us.

CHAINS ✦ Chains in a line can indicate obstacles. So if there are chains early in a life line, that can mean a difficult childhood.

CROSSES ✦ Suggesting stress, crosses are more pronounced than grilles—this is more along the lines of "a cross to bear."

FRAY ✦ When a line ends in a fray, that indicates confusion. The life line often ends in this way.

GRILLES ✦ These can indicate stress.

ISLANDS ✦ An island represents an interruption that is more significant than a break; it is generally a difficult time.

TRIDENT, TRIANGLE ✦ These markings are considered signs of good luck.

CHIROGNOMY

Chirognomy looks at the shape of the hands, grouping them into four distinct categories, based on the four elements. It also looks at the individual fingers, the thumb, the fingernails, the size of the hands, and their texture. You'll note that chirognomy is pretty black-and-white in its interpretations, and that having short fingers is pretty much always a bad thing. Chirognomy is only somewhat useful and so is often just incorporated into a general palmistry practice to enhance the reading of the lines.

hand shape
✳

THE FIRE HAND: Short fingers and a relatively long palm. This person is extroverted and outgoing, and also fairly emotional.

THE EARTH HAND: Short fingers and a square palm. Practical, hardworking, and somewhat resistant to change. Prefers a life spent out-of-doors.

THE AIR HAND: Long fingers, square palm. Logical, intelligent, good communicator, but easily bored.

THE WATER HAND: Long fingers, long palm. Sensitive and creative, driven by their emotions. May not handle stress well.

hand size
✳

LARGE: Proportionally larger hands indicate that the person is capable, hardworking, and sociable.

SMALL: Proportionally smaller hands indicate that the person can be a little egotistical and quite ambitious.

AVERAGE: Those who fall in between have a lot of common sense and show good judgment.

hand texture

THICK: Stubborn, somewhat insensitive.

THIN: Sensitive—hence, thin-skinned.

ROUGH: Hardworking, practical, somewhat impatient—i.e., doesn't use lotion.

SOFT: Artistic, refined—i.e., uses lotion.

fingers

Note that the length of each finger should be measured in relation to the others, rather than based on actual length. For example, someone with a small hand but a relatively long index finger would be more confident and capable than someone with a larger hand (and therefore a larger index finger) but whose index finger is shorter in relation to their other fingers.

INDEX FINGER: Also known as the Jupiter Finger. Long indicates that the person is confident and capable; short signifies shy and lacking in self-confidence.

MIDDLE FINGER: Also known as the Saturn Finger. Long suggests the person is hardworking and detail-oriented; short communicates that the person isn't particularly ambitious, but is willing to take risks.

RING FINGER: Also known as the Apollo Finger. Long reveals that the person is creative and artistic; short tells us that the person might lack enthusiasm.

PINKIE FINGER: Also known as the Mercury Finger. Long indicates that the person is highly intelligent and a good communicator; short implies that the person might be immature.

THUMB: A large thumb generally signifies that the person is a leader, while a small thumb means the person is more of a follower. A hitchhiker's thumb (a thumb that can bend over backward) means that the person is easygoing, while a rigid thumb means the person is—you guessed it—rigid.

fingertips

✦

CONE-SHAPED: Flexible and willing to compromise.

POINTED: Sensitive, artistic.

SPATULATE (flaring outward): Creative, inventive, pioneering.

SQUARE: Methodical and rational.

fingernails

✦

THIN AND CURVED: Gentle, kind.

BROAD: Strong personality, might have a temper.

FAN-SHAPED: Stressed.

HOW TO DO A READING

Start with the person's nondominant hand, as this will provide a baseline for you to read the differences in the dominant hand. Take your time—there is a lot to absorb. Take notes if you want or need to.

Next, look at the person's dominant hand. For now, don't worry about comparing the two, just see what the dominant hand tells you. Again, take notes if you need to.

Finally, look at the differences between the two. If lines are clearer on one hand than the other, what does that say to you? If some markings are present on one hand, but not the other, what does that imply? For instance, if the fate line is present on the nondominant hand, but is missing on the dominant hand, perhaps that person has—for better or worse—stepped aside from their destiny.

Don't forget to look at the shapes of the hands to see what chirognomy adds to your information.

When you feel confident that you have learned all that you can, share your understanding with the person whose hands you have been studying. Walk them through the process, and see how much of it rings true.

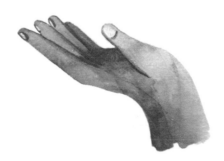

DREAM
INTERPRETATION

· ·

WE ALL DREAM. WE MAY NOT ALL REMEMBER OUR DREAMS, BUT
we all dream. And sometimes our dreams are pretty weird, and we wake up
wondering what on earth our unconscious/the Divine/our past selves were trying to tell us. There are dreams so intense we feel they *must* be significant.

The specifics of how and why we dream are still unclear, but oneirologists
(dream scientists) agree that dreams help us form memories, process emotions, and sort through the events of the day. Some folks believe that dreams are
messages sent to us from the beyond or that they reflect events that occurred in
past lives. There are traditions of dream interpretations in Islam, Christianity,
Hinduism, and Buddhism, with many overlapping symbols.

And, of course, dreams play a huge role in psychology and psychother-
apy. Sigmund Freud believed that dreams are the "royal road" to the unconscious, and if we could decode them, we could understand our true natures.
Symbols are the language of dreams, and it's believed that everything in our
dreams has a specific meaning. But while a dream dictionary could tell you
that dreaming of a fern symbolizes one's hopes and fears for the future, it
might not necessarily mean that for you specifically. You might dream of a
fern because your grandmother kept ferns in her house and you're missing
her, or for any number of reasons that are specific to you.

Still, oneirologists have noticed trends and similar dreams that happen to almost every one of us at some point (often more than once) in different cultures all over the world. Dreams of going to school naked, or flying, or falling are clichés for a reason, because we all have them so often. And because they are so common, we are able to interpret them in a fairly consistent fashion. In the same way that yawning can be interpreted as sleepiness and a smile can be interpreted as happiness regardless of who is doing the yawning or the smiling, these common dreams have reliable interpretations for everyone.

On the other hand, while the less common dream symbols aren't nearly as reliable, they can be useful. Those disturbing dreams that just won't let us go can be released with understanding, and an understanding of dream symbols can provide us with a jumping-off point, a way to begin to interpret them. Dream dictionaries have thousands of symbols, some of them as common as mothers, and some as esoteric as ice makers. Who dreams about ice makers? But if you do, then you should know that means that you are shutting others out, closing yourself off from your relationships—whether you feel this applies to you or not, it is food for thought.

Dreams have meaning, and if we look at them closely, we can decipher them as best we can, so that we may further understand ourselves.

COMMON DREAM SYMBOLS

Most likely, you've dreamed each of these at least once.

BABIES ✦ Dreaming of a baby/dreaming of being pregnant may be driven by your body's biological desire to procreate, or it may mean that you want or need to be nurtured yourself. It may also signify a new idea.

BEING CHASED ✦ We tend to remember these dreams because the anxiety we feel during them is extremely vivid. Take a look at what's chasing you to interpret the dream—because of course whatever it is you're running away from is really the issue at hand. What is it you don't want to face in your life? Your dream is telling you to *stop running*.

DEATH ✦ As in tarot, these dreams do not portend literal death. You need not be worried that you are ill or that someone you love is in danger. Instead, they signal that you are at the start or in the middle of a big change—an ending of one thing and a new beginning of another.

FALLING ✦ Normally, falling indicates anxiety that comes after success. Once you've achieved what you wanted, how will you maintain it?

FLYING ✦ This is almost invariably a euphoric dream, and it often occurs once we've finally made a decision we've been putting off or when we're feeling particularly confident that we can achieve our goals.

NUDITY ✦ We've all suffered from the "forgot your clothes" dream. This generally unpleasant dream signifies how vulnerable you are feeling. You may want to consider baring yourself regardless of your fear. Get it over with and really put your true self out there for the world to see.

PEOPLE ✦ Just about everyone dreams about other people, but the important thing to note is that each of the "characters" in our dreams represents some aspect of ourselves.

SEX ◆ Along with just being good fun, sex dreams indicate that you have reached a new level of understanding and incorporated the intuitive with the conscious.

TEST YOU DIDN'T STUDY FOR ◆ These dreams aren't actually an argument against the stressors of the Common Core. Instead, they indicate that you are examining yourself, looking at past mistakes.

OUT-OF-CONTROL VEHICLE ◆ You know that dream—the one where the brakes don't work or the steering wheel won't turn? It's telling you that you're trying too hard to control something that you simply don't have control over. Relax the white-knuckle grip and let the road take you where it will.

WATER ◆ Water is generally thought to speak specifically to the state of the unconscious. If you're dreaming of a stormy sea, you may be experiencing some emotional turbulence. But if you're dreaming of a cool, clear stream, you are more likely experiencing mental clarity.

LESS COMMON
(But Still Fairly Common)
DREAM SYMBOLS

These are less common—but still experienced more often than an ice maker—and can generally be relied upon to have some relevance to most of us.

NEEDING TO GO TO THE BATHROOM ✦ This probably just means that you need to go to the bathroom, but it could also mean that you ought to consider looking after your own needs, instead of always putting others first.

CELEBRITIES ✦ When a celebrity pops up in your dream, they can indicate a certain admiration. Perhaps that celebrity has a quality that you would like to embody.

CHEATING BY YOUR SIGNIFICANT OTHER ✦ This dream often leaves us angry at our partners, though we know we have no just cause. It doesn't indicate a problem in the relationship; instead you may be feeling insecure or in need of a little extra care and attention.

CHEATING YOURSELF ✦ If you are the one having an affair in a dream, remember that doesn't mean anything about your feelings for your partner. Instead, look at the person you are cheating with. What aspects of their personality do you find attractive?

FOOD ✦ Dreaming of food can mean that you are hungry, but it can also symbolize a hunger for knowledge.

HAIR ✦ According to Freud, hair is symbolic of sexuality (but then so many things were, to Freud). Abundant hair equates with sexual abundance and virility, while hair loss speaks of a loss of libido.

HOUSE ◆ Each room or floor of a house in a dream has a meaning that is specific to the dreamer, but generally a basement represents that which is ignored and a bedroom represents that which is private.

KILLING ◆ If you kill someone in your dreams, that doesn't make you a violent person. Remember that every character in your dream represents a part of yourself. What part of yourself are you trying to kill off?

PARALYSIS ◆ When we are in a REM sleep state, we are actually paralyzed to an extent—which is a good thing, as it prevents us from sleepwalking and acting out the experiences in our dreams. When we are in the midst of waking up while in that state, we can experience that paralysis for a moment. So this isn't really a dream symbol, but an actual state of being.

SNAKE ◆ The symbolism of snakes in dreams depends on your personal feelings about snakes. If you dislike them or are afraid of them, they may speak to a hidden or unpredictable threat. But they can also represent healing, transformation, and creativity. And of course, according to Freud, they represent sexual temptation.

TEETH FALLING OUT ◆ Teeth symbolize confidence and power. Ask yourself, what are you feeling powerless about? We also use them to communicate—what are you unable to voice?

HOW TO INTERPRET DREAMS

Start by keeping a dream journal. Record every dream you remember when you first wake up in the morning, before it fades, making note of any details that jump out at you. Pay particular attention to recurring dreams, including recurring dream locations, as those have particular significance for your psyche.

At the end of the day, before you go to sleep, write about what's on your mind. This is just good sense in its own right—by getting the stresses of your day out of your head and onto the page, you make it more likely that you'll have a restful sleep. But it will also enable you to see how the events of the day or days leading up to your dreams shaped those dreams.

Over time, you will notice patterns, and symbols that repeat will make their meanings clear to you.

If you're interpreting someone else's dream, listen carefully and patiently. Other people's dreams are never as interesting as our own, but do your best. If you notice any particular symbols, make note of them. Feel free to ask questions about what might be going on in their life, so that you can interpret more clearly. When you do offer your interpretation, make clear that this isn't an exact science, and this is only your take on it—dreams are very personal, and even if someone has asked you to interpret, they may not like what you have to say. Even so, give your honest opinion, and don't try to make light of a negative dream.

LUCID DREAMS

Technically, a lucid dream is defined as a dream in which the dreamer is aware that they are dreaming. But that's not all we think of when we hear the words "lucid dreaming." We think of *controlling* our dreams, and while of course that requires knowing that we are dreaming in the first place, let's just for the sake of simplicity say that lucid dreaming equals controlling your dreams.

Why would you want to do that? Well, for starters, it's really *fun*. You can do anything you want! You can fly, you can work magic, you can live an elaborate love story, you can save the world. But you can also help yourself. Lucid dreaming is obviously extremely helpful for people who suffer from nightmares, and it can be a powerful healing process, both emotionally and physically. We all know that when we're sick, visualizing our bodies as healthy is an effective way to promote healing. If we take that to the next level by dreaming about ourselves as healthy, think how much more powerful that healing could be.

The first step toward lucid dreaming is becoming aware that you are dreaming while it is happening. Keeping a dream journal will help with this, as will simply paying attention to your dreams, granting them space in your waking mind. Work on remembering them. When you wake up from a dream, even if it is the middle of the night, take the time to write it down, or at the very least go over it in your mind from start to finish, working to recall as many details as you can, so you can write it down at a later time.

The best time to lucid dream is when you are just barely asleep—in the early morning hours, say, or during a nap. Your awareness is strong enough that you can realize you are sleeping, and with that awareness, you give yourself agency in the dream. Once you've improved your dream recall, try this method of lucid dreaming: If you wake up out of a dream in the early morning, pay attention to that dream as closely as you can, while still allowing your mind to stay in its relaxed state. Daydream the dream over again. And then, once you've found a way you wish to direct the dream, allow yourself to fall back asleep. It may be a very light sleep, but you will find yourself dreaming the daydream.

This method of slow, gentle initiation into lucid dreaming usually results in an effective lucid dream, but there are other methods. Sometimes, you realize you are dreaming mid-dream but have no ability to affect the dream. This can be quite frustrating, but that sense of helplessness will dissolve with time and practice—remember, just like in *The Matrix*, "there is no spoon." You do have control, and you can do anything.

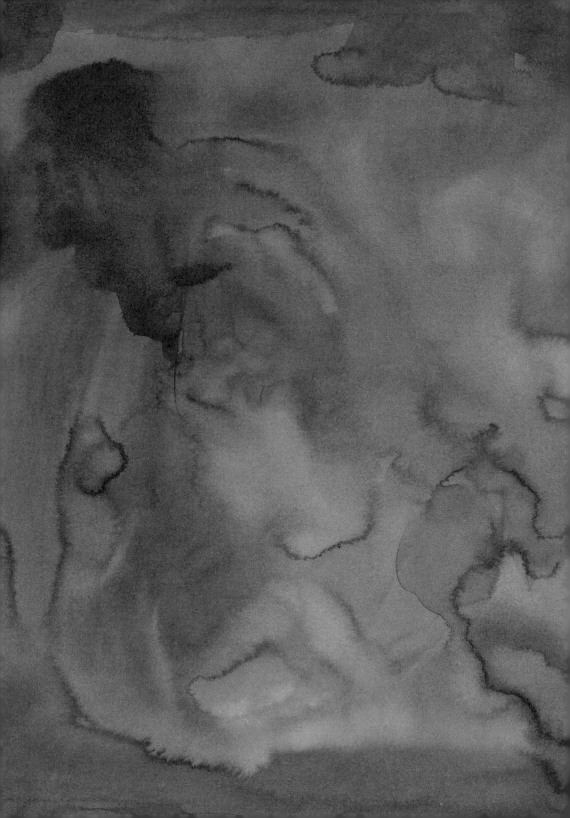

CONCLUSION

IF YOU CHOSE TO PICK UP THIS BOOK, THEN YOU WERE PROBABLY already interested and perhaps already knew some of the information contained here. So some chapters may have had you nodding sagely, gaining a deeper understanding of herbal healing or astrology or chakras. And some chapters may have had you thinking to yourself, "this is a load of hooey"— which is totally fine!

The best chapters are the ones that you *didn't* already find interesting before you started, that you looked at with skepticism. But you read them anyway, and you came out on the other side wondering— *what if?* What if auras are a real thing, even if we can't see them yet ourselves? What if tarot can help us understand truths within ourselves that we might not otherwise be able to see?

If you accept and embrace the concept of chakras, then using crystals to aid in chakra based healing just makes sense. It is a very short leap from herbal healing to herbal magic, so short the two are almost indistinguishable. And while our Western culture doesn't generally celebrate pagan holidays anymore, they are at the root of so many holidays we *do* celebrate that their traditions are both joyous and fun.

That's all we're hoping for here—a little curiosity, a willingness to ask, "what if?" If you chuckle at the idea of doing spells, but can't imagine yourself actually sitting and casting one without dying of embarrassment, then spells are not the right kind of magic for you! But if you find yourself better able to understand your own dreams—and therefore deal with the issues your subconscious is struggling with—then, for all practical purposes, that, too, is magic.

Pull that tarot card, and see what it says. Study the lines on your palm to gain greater self-knowledge. What can your natal chart tell you about yourself, about the ways you react to certain kinds of situations, and how can you use that information to live your life with greater ease?

And if you do all that, is it magic? Is any of this magic? If chakras are rooted in an early understanding of the human endocrine system, are they, in fact, science? If you cast a healing spell on your best friend and she gets better, was that you or was it her immune system?

Perhaps the question ought to be—does it matter? If we do no harm, and perhaps even some good, then all that matters is what we believe is possible. If we simply allow for the possibility of magic, it can become real, practical, and true. We make it so, and so mote it be.

REFERENCES AND RESOURCES

There is a lot of information on a lot of topics in this book, and therefore, none of that information goes into all that much depth. If you're curious to know more about any particular topic, check out these useful links and books for a greater understanding!

astrology

The Astrology Bible by Judy Hall. Sterling Publishing, April 2005.

The Only Astrology Book You'll Ever Need by Joanne Martine Woolfolk. Taylor Trade Publishing, November 2012.

Astrolabe, https://alabe.com/freechart

Astrology, http://www.astrology.com.tr/birth-chart.asp

Astrology Zone, https://www.astrologyzone.com/learn-astrology

Horoscope, http://www.horoscope.com/us/index.aspx

auras

Change Your Aura, Change Your Life by Barbara Y. Martin & Dimitri Moraitis. Tarcher, April 2016.

The Unseen Self: Kirlian Photography, Explained by Brian Snellgrove. Random House UK, December 2004

Psychic Library, http://psychiclibrary.com/beyondBooks/aura-room

chakras

✴

The Book of Chakras: Discovering the Hidden Forces Within You by Ambika Wauters. Barron's, April 2002.

Chakra Anatomy, http://www.chakra-anatomy.com/index.html

The Chopra Center, http://www.chopra.com/articles/what-is-a-chakra

Modern Chakra, http://www.modernchakra.com/chakra-science.html

crystals

✴

The Crystal Bible by Judy Hall. Walking Stick Press, May 2003.

Crystals for Healing by Karen Frazier. Althea Press, November 2015.

Crystal Vaults, https://www.crystalvaults.com/crystal-encyclopedia/crystal-guide

Healing Crystals, https://www.healingcrystals.com/The_Healing_Power_of_ Crystals_Articles_1115.html

dream interpretation

Dreamer's Dictionary by Stearn Robinson & Tom Corbett. Grand Central Publishing, February 1986.

Exploring the World of Lucid Dreaming by Stephen LaBerge & Howard Rheingold. Ballantine Publishing, November 1991.

Dream Moods, http://www.dreammoods.com/dreamdictionary

Lucidity, http://www.lucidity.com/LucidDreamingFAQ2.html

herbs

The Herbal Apothecary by JJ Pursell. Timber, December 2015.

The Modern Herbal Dispensatory by Thomas Easley & Steven Home. North Atlantic, November 2016.

Learning Herbs, http://learningherbs.com/free-herbal-remedies

Mountain Rose Herbs, https://www.mountainroseherbs.com

Wellness Mama, https://wellnessmama.com/category/remedies

pagan holidays

The Pagan Book of Days by Nigel Pennick. Destiny Books, March 2001.

Circle Sanctuary, https://www.circlesanctuary.org/index.php/celebrating-the-seasons/celebrating-the-seasons

Wicca, https://wicca.com/celtic/akasha/index0.htm

palmistry

The Art and Science of Hand Reading by Ellen Goldberg. Destiny Books, February 2016.

The Palmistry Bible by Jane Struthers. Sterling Publishing, August 2005.

Palmistry, http://www.palmistry.com.au/palmistry.html

Psychic Library, http://psychiclibrary.com/beyondBooks/palmistry-room

plant-based magic

Herb Magic for Beginners by Ellen Dugan. Llewellyn, May 2006.

Secret Recipes from your Garden by Ellen Evert Hopman. Healing Arts Press, February 2016.

Witches Lore, http://witcheslore.com/bookofshadows/herbology/plant-and-herb-magic-2/1174

Witchipedia, http://www.witchipedia.com/main:herbs

tarot

The Ultimate Guide to Tarot by Liz Dean. Fair Winds Press, May 2015.

Biddy Tarot, https://www.biddytarot.com/tarot-card-meanings

Psychic Library, http://psychiclibrary.com/beyondBooks/tarot-deck

white magic

Buckland's Complete Book of Witchcraft by Raymond Buckland. Llewllyn, 2002.

The Modern Guide to Witchcraft by Skye Alexander. Adams Media, July 2014.

Spells of Magic, http://www.spellsofmagic.com/white_magic.html

Wiccan Spells, http://wiccanspells.info

Witches Lore, http://witcheslore.com/category/spells

ACKNOWLEDGMENTS

SO MANY PEOPLE ARE RESPONSIBLE FOR THIS BOOK. Shannon Connors, for being the most lovely Wicca-curious, kombucha-making, light-bringing editorfriend you could be. Katie Vernon for illustrations so beautiful and evocative they make my heart skip. Susan Van Horn for a gorgeous design—you make my many bullet points look good. Kristin Kiser for keeping me so happy and so busy. Ashley Benning for some light copyediting. Kelly Notaras for introducing me to this world that I am so happy to be dwelling in. Chandika Devi and Rachel Mehl for never yelling at me when I was overwhelmed. David Dunton for saying "Yay!" all those times I demanded he do so. Maile Dunton for being so psyched about everything all the time. I love you all.

CREATING YOUR NATAL CHART

For a real, in-depth natal chart—one that calculates angles of ascension and how the signs and planets interact with each other—go to the professionals (and there are lots of websites that will do your chart for free). But you can dive in yourself for just a taste and to take a look at how the signs influence the houses.

① On the opposite page you will find a chart, with three concentric circles, divided into twelve equal slices.

② Determine your ascendant sign. This sign is whatever was rising over the horizon on the date and at the exact time of your birth. Find it by looking it up in an ephemeris (a chart that tracks the positions of celestial bodies at any given time) or by looking it up online. Position this information at eight o'clock on your chart. This is your First House (The House of Self).

③ Follow the natural order of the signs (Aries, Taurus, Gemini, Cancer, Leo, Virgo, Libra, Scorpio, Sagittarius, Capricorn, Aquarius, Pisces) as you fill in each of the remaining eleven spaces. So if you had Aries in your First House, you would put Taurus in the Second House, Gemini in the Third House, and so forth.

For more information on the significance of your natal chart, see page 112.

INDEX

a

abundance spell, 82
agate, yellow, 75
air signs, 102, 105
ajna, 16, 19, 22
amethyst, 22, 23, 68, 71
anahata, 15, 19, 22
angelica, 68
apples, 74
aquamarine, 22, 23, 61, 84
Aquarius, 102, 105
Aries, 102, 103
ascendant signs, 112, 146
ashwagandha, 43
astral aura, 30
astrological charts, 102
astrology
    celestial bodies, 107–109
    creating a natal chart, 112, 146
    elements and their signs, 103–106
    overview of, 101–102
    references and resources for, 141
    twelve houses, 110–111
auras
    cleansing, 36–37
    common colors and meanings for, 32–35
    how to see, 36
    layers of, 30–31
    overview of, 29–31
    references and resources for, 141
azurite, 22, 23, 84

b

balance, 12, 15, 17–19, 55
banishing spell, 83
basil, 68
bay laurel, 68
bayberry, 67

belladonna, 57, 65, 83
Beltane, 71
betony, 57, 60, 78, 82
black, 35, 65
black cohosh, 43
bloodstone, 68
blue, 16, 34, 71
body-mind connection, 11
botanomancy, 56
Brighid, 68
brown, 74, 75
burning bush, 45

c

calcite, 23, 61, 83
calendula, 44
Cancer, 102, 106
Capricorn, 102, 104
caraway, 57, 60, 61, 85
carnelian, 22, 23, 26, 61, 74, 85
casting, 79
catnip, 44, 65
celestial bodies, 107–109
celestial aura, 31
chakras
    balancing, 17–19
    main, 13–17
    overview of, 11–12
    references and resources for, 142
chamomile, 71, 72
chirognomy, 116, 124–126
Chirological Society of Great Britain, 115
chiromancy, 116, 117–123
chunk crystals, 25
cinquefoil, 57, 60, 61, 78, 82
circles, 78, 79
citrine, 22, 23, 61, 82, 84
clear quartz, 22, 23, 26–27, 78, 81

clover, 57, 84
colors, 32–35, 61. *see also individual colors*
cowslip, 57
cranberry, 44–45
crown chakra, 17, 22
crystals
 chakras and, 18, 22
 choosing and activating, 25–27
 clearing, 26
 common, 23–24
 overview of, 21–22
 references and resources for, 142
 shapes of, 25–26
Cups, 89, 91
cut crystals, 25

d

"deadly nightshade," 57
Destiny, Line of, 120
diamond, 67
dittany, 45
dragon's blood, 57, 60, 61, 85
dream journals, 135, 136
dreams
 how to interpret, 135
 lucid, 136–137
 overview of interpretation of, 129–130
 references and resources for, 142
 symbols from, 131–134

e

earth signs, 102, 104
elderberry, 45
elecampane, 57, 83
electromagnetic photography, 30
elemental categories, 102, 103–106
elements and their signs, 103–106
emerald, 67, 70, 72, 74
emotional aura, 30
Eostre, 69–70
essential oils, 18, 52
etheric aura, 30

etheric template aura, 30
evergreen, 67
eyebright, 57

f

felt, 61
feverfew, 46
fingernails, 126
fingers, size and shape of, 125–126
fire signs, 102, 103
flight, plants for, 57, 58
frankincense, 57
frequencies, of chakras, 12
Freud, Sigmund, 129

g

garlic, 58, 60, 61, 79, 81, 82, 83
garnet, 22, 23, 67, 68, 81
Gemini, 102, 105
giving thanks, 79
gold, 35, 67, 72, 75
golden calcite, 22
grains, 74
green, 15, 33, 67, 70, 71, 72, 74
Green Man, 70, 74
gris-gris, 60
guidance spread, 99

h

hands, shape and size of, 124–126. *see also* palmistry
hawthorn, 58, 60, 79, 85
head line, 119
healing spell, 81
heart chakra, 15
heart line, 118
hellebore, 58, 61, 83
hematite, 22, 23, 65, 82, 83
henbane, 58, 61
herb of grace, 49

herbs. *see also* plant-based magic
  common, 43–51
  making a tincture from, 52
  making oil with, 52–53
  making poultice with, 53
  overview of, 41–42
  references and resources for, 143
holidays. *see* pagan holidays
holly, 56, 58, 67, 79
honeysuckle, 58, 60, 61, 82, 85
hops, 74
horse chestnut, 46–47
Houses, 102
Houses (astrology), 110–111
hyssop, 58, 60, 78, 83

i

Imbolc, 68–69
indigo, chakras and, 16
intention, role of, 56
invocation, 79
islands (palmistry), 123

j

jade, 22, 23, 61, 82, 85
jasper, 70
jet, 65
juniper, 58
Jupiter, 108

k

ketheric template aura, 31
Kirlian photography, 30

l

Lammas, 73–74
lapis lazuli, 22, 24, 61, 75, 83
lavender, 58, 61, 71, 72, 84
leather, 61
lemon balm, 47, 58, 61, 85
Leo, 102, 103

Libra, 102, 105
life line, 117–118
light frequencies of chakras, 12
Litha, 72–73
love spells, 57, 58, 59, 85
Lugh, 74

m

Mabon, 75
Major Arcana, 94–97
malachite, 22, 24
mandrake, 58, 60, 65, 79, 82, 84, 85
manipura, 14, 19, 22
marigold, 44, 58, 60, 61, 75, 82
marjoram, 58
markings, on hand, 123
Mars, 108
marshmallow, 47
meditation, 17–18, 57
melissa (herb), 47
mental aura, 30
Mercury, 107
milk thistle, 48, 67, 75
milkweed, 75
Minor Arcana, 89
mistletoe, 58, 60, 61, 67, 85
Moon, 107
moonstone, 24, 84
mounts, 121–122
mugwort, 59, 61, 65, 72, 83
muladhara, 13, 18, 22
mullein, 48–49
myrtle, 59, 60, 61, 79, 85

n

natal chart, creating, 112, 146
Neptune, 109

o

obsidian, 22, 24, 65, 82, 83, 84
oils, herbal, 52–53

oneirologists (dream scientists), 129–130
opal, 24, 61, 83
orange, 14, 33, 65, 74, 75
Ostara, 69–70

p

pagan holidays
    descriptions of, 65–75
    overview of, 63–64
    references and resources for, 143
palmistry
    chirognomy, 124–126
    chiromancy, 117–123
    how to do a reading using, 127
    overview of, 115–116
    references and resources for, 143
Pentacles, 89, 92
pentagrams, 77, 78
peridot, 71
peripheral vision, 36
pimpernel, 59, 80
pink, 32, 68
Pisces, 102, 106
plantain leaf, 49
plant-based magic. *see also* herbs
    common plants and their uses, 57–59
    gris-gris, 61
    overview of, 55–56
    references and resources for, 144
    smudge sticks, 60
Pluto, 109
poultices, 53
prana, 11
protection, 79
protection spell, 82
Ptolemy, 101
purification, 78
purple, 17, 34, 71
pyrite, 24, 82

q

quartz, 22, 23, 24, 25, 26–27, 61, 78, 79, 81, 82, 85

r

red, 13, 32, 67, 68, 75
references and resources, 141–144
ritual space, creating, 78
root chakra, 13, 22
rose quartz, 22, 24, 61, 79, 85
rosemary, 59, 60
ruby, 67
rue, 49
Rule of Three, 77

s

sabbats. *see* pagan holidays
sacra chakra, 13–14, 22
sage, 59, 60, 65, 75, 81, 84, 85
Sagittarius, 102, 103
sahasrara, 17, 19, 22
salt circles, 78
Samhain, 65–66
sapphire, 71, 75
Saturn, 108–109
Scorpio, 102, 106
self-confidence spell, 84
silver, 35, 65, 67
smoky quartz, 22, 24, 82, 85
smudge sticks, 60
solar plexus chakra, 14, 22
Solomon's seal, 75
spells, 55–56, 77–85
St. John's wort, 59, 60, 61, 83
subtle bodies, 30–31
suits of tarot, 89, 91–93
summoning spell, 83
Sun, 107
Sun God, 72, 74
sun line, 120
svadhisthana, 13–14, 19, 22

Swords, 89, 92–93

symbols, dreams and, 131–134

t

Tailte, 74

tansy, 68

tarot

    guidance spread, 99

    Major Arcana, 94–97

    overview of, 89–90

    references and resources for, 144

    suits of, 89, 91–93

    three-card spread, 98

Taurus, 102, 104

Tetrabiblos (Ptolemy), 101

texture, hand, 125

third eye chakra, 16, 22

three-card spread, 98

throat chakra, 15–16, 22

thyme, 59, 60, 72, 82, 84

tiger's eye, 24, 61, 80

tinctures, 52

truth spell, 80

tumbled crystals, 26

turmeric, 41

turquoise, 22, 24, 81

twelve houses, 110–111

u

Uranus, 109

v

valerian, 50

velvet, 61

Venus, 108

vervain, 50–51, 56, 59, 60, 72, 78, 82

Virgo, 102, 104

vishuddha, 15–16, 19, 22

w

wand crystals, 26

Wands, 89, 93

water signs, 102, 106

white, 35, 65, 68

white magic, 77–85, 144

willow bark, 41

wormwood, 59, 61, 71, 83

y

yarrow, 51, 59, 61, 72, 83

yellow, 14, 33, 68, 70, 72, 74

yellow agate, 75

yellow jasper, 22, 24

Yule, 66–67

z

zodiac, 102

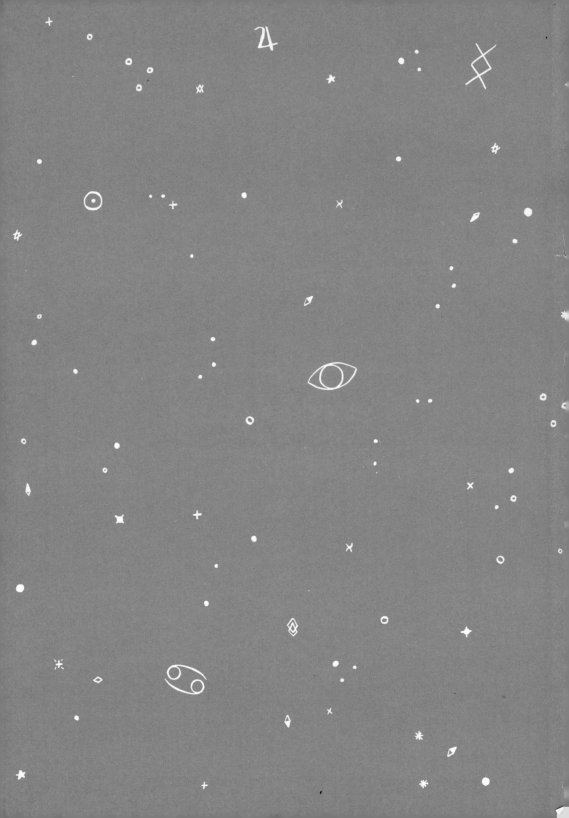